The Book of Clare

Paintings by Tomás O'Maoldomhnaigh
Text by Daniel McCarthy

First published by Cottage Publications,
an imprint of Laurel Cottage Ltd.
Donaghadee, N. Ireland 2003.

Design & origination in Northern Ireland.
Printed & bound in Singapore.

ISBN 1 90093533 3

Daniel McCarthy

Daniel McCarthy is the author of the critically acclaimed, *Ireland's Banner County*, (2002). He holds a Masters Degree in History from N.U.I. Galway and has worked in various Irish museums for a number of years.

He presently runs the heritage consultancy service, Boru Cultural Enterprises, which specialises in heritage marketing and historical research and exhibitions, offering innovative historical-based communications solutions to dynamic organisations.

He was 'bred in New York, buttered in Lissycasey' where, through the local club, he developed a lifelong passion for Gaelic football. Today he lives in Cragbrien, Darragh, County Clare, with his wife Siobhán and children, Seán, Laura and Donal Óg.

Tomás O'Maoldomhnaigh

Tomás O'Maoldomhnaigh, born 1956 is a self-taught artist. He has exhibited in group Exhibitions since 1977 with Limerick Art Society. He is an active member of both the Market Artists Group and the Clare Association of Artists & Craftpersons.

Tomás has built a reputation for his many paintings in the area of industrial portraiture. His works can be found all over Ireland and are displayed by many of Irelands top companies. He exhibits on an on-going basis in the Mid West although he paints mostly commissioned work in his studio in Ennis. His paintings have been sold to the United States, Europe, Africa and Australia.

Although a noted portrait painter, County Clare and the west of Ireland provide inspirational material for his paintings. He now lives and works as a full time artist and illustrator in his adopted County Clare with his wife Caroline and their two boys, Patrick and Brendan.

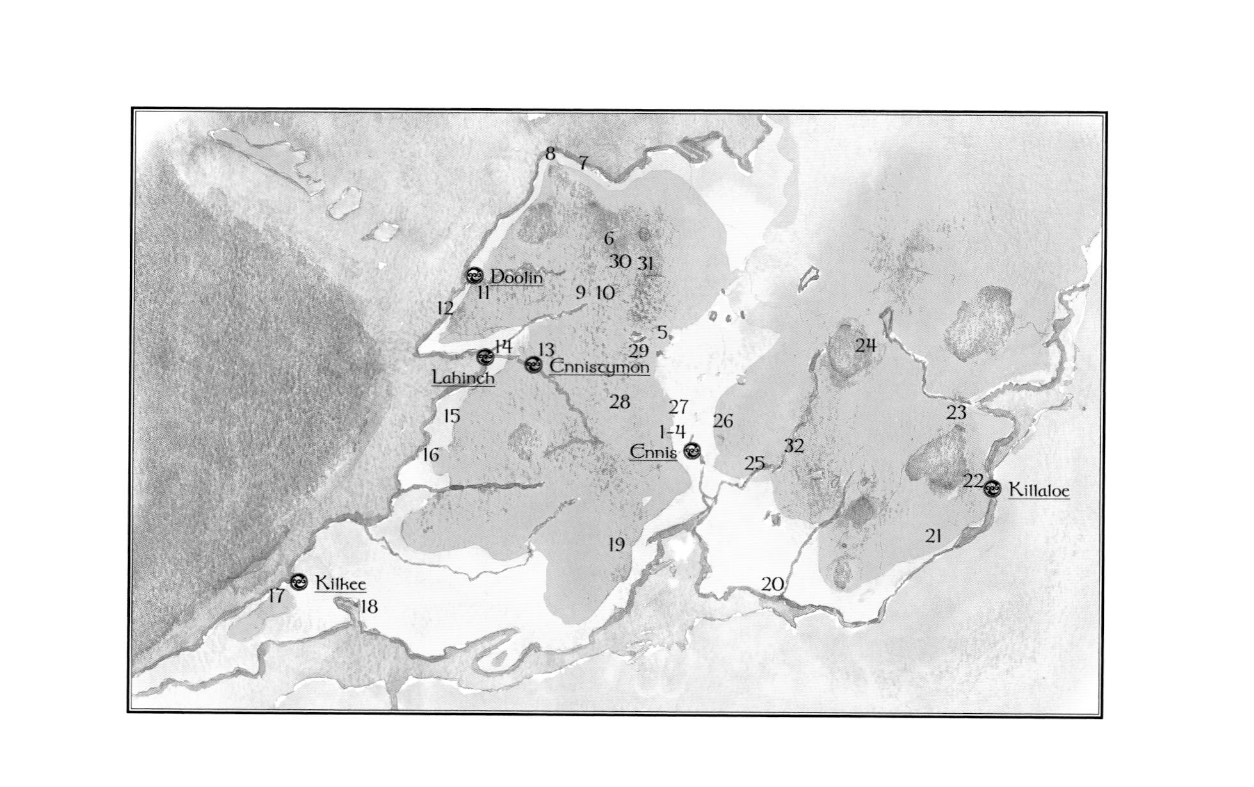

8
7
6
30
31
Doolin
11
9
10
12
5
14
13
29
Lahinch
Ennistymon
24
28
27
15
26
1-4
23
Ennis
32
16
25
22
Killaloe
21
19
Kilkee
20
17
18

Contents

The Spirit of Clare

Clare is a state of mind. It is a mood. It takes you along from the soothing embrace of the Shannon River which hugs its eastern and southern borders, intersected only by the island-studded Fergus estuary, to the thunderous Atlantic which crashes against the sturdy western face of Clare, a face that has in more than one sense, always looked outward. It brings you to its northern expanses where nestling off Galway Bay are over 259 square kilometres of dramatic limestone karst landscape known as the Burren, which was largely sculpted by God and his glaciers 15,000 years ago. The omnipresent stone-built monuments whisper of a civilization whose architecture was more ancient than that of the Egyptian pyramids.

It drifts through the continental time-gaps of the Devonian and Silurian periods and the high, boggy wilds of Ballycrom Hill between Feakle and Caher, overlooking Lough Graney where the women of Ireland held the fairy court with the poet, Brian Merriman in his 18th century vision, *Cúirt an Mheánoíche.* And on it goes through the rugged hills, idyllic valleys and woodlands of East Clare to the shores of Lough Derg, where residing nearby in regal splendour at Raheen Wood in Tuamgraney for reputedly over a millennium, is the magnificent Brian Boru Oak Tree, one of Ireland's greatest living specimens. Close by, people still worship in the oldest continuously used church in western Europe, the same ecclesiastical surrounds within which Boru, Imperatoris Scotorum, the 'Emperor of the Irish' as ascribed to him by the Book of Armagh, did pray. Then you are brought to the heartland and you feel its history, its folklore and its faith at every pulse. Quin Abbey, founded by the McNamaras in 1350 and incorporating the original castle structure built by Richard de Clare in 1280 and its resting occupant, John 'Fireball' McNamara, who in his prime carried a pistol known as *Bás gan sagart* – death without priest. Dromore, with its castle and nature reserve, O'Brien's Castle, near Spancilhill, built by the Bishop of Killaloe and later occupied by Cromwell's troops. Mooghaun, wherein is located Ireland's largest archaeological site and where also was discovered the greatest prehistoric gold hoard in the western world outside of the Aegean civilization. There are the storied sites of Magowna, Dysert O'Dea, Clare Abbey, Islandmagrath and Ben Dash.

To the west you see the weather-beaten open plains and peninsulas, the broad streets of landlord Kilrush kept sentry over by the monastic Inis Cathaigh (better known by the Norse-derived name of Scattery Island), where God-fearing monks, relic-seeking Vikings and revenge-seeking chieftains all held sway in turn. The chest expands and nostrils flare with the salt sea breezes that extend across the beaches, sand dunes and golf links of Kilkee, White Strand, Doughmore, Seafield, Spanish Point, Lahinch and Fanore. Located just north of Lahinch on the coast of West Clare, are the Cliffs of Moher. Natural ramparts against the might of the Atlantic, they rise in places to over 215m and stretch for almost 8km. And then you are at the county seat of Inis Cluain Ramh-Fhada, Ennis, and the focal point of Clare. The hub of a radial route network, its winding y-shaped medieval street patterns are juxtaposed with its standing today as the Information Age Town. Its name, its location and its development were all influenced by the two forces of nature, the Fergus River and the O'Brien family, the ancient blueblood of Clare. The O'Briens established their principal seat here at Clonroad around 1208 as the Normans swept into Munster. Enshrined within the very foundation of Ennis was a tradition of hospitality. It was at the behest of Donnchadh Cairbreach O'Brien that a group of friars, who had wandered into the vicinity around 1241, established an Abbey of St. Francis. Ennis Abbey itself, the imposing national monument that is a dominant feature of the town skyline, dates back to the 1280s.

Clare is a county of antiquity. Once a native principality called Tuath-Mumhan, (Thomond, signifying "North Munster"), this peninsular 'island' county was peopled by the ruling septs of O'Brien, MacNamara, McMahon, O'Dea, O'Loughlin, Uí Chormaic and O'Gorman. The Site Monument Records of The National Monuments Services list at least 2,300 earthen and stone forts, 130 megalithic tombs, 190 castles, 150 ancient churches, 3 cathedrals, 8 monasteries, 10 stone crosses, 5 round towers, besides numerous lesser monuments located throughout the county, approximately 6,000 national monuments in Clare in total. Such an abundance of archaeological remains testify to the vitality and ingenuity of Clare's ancestral inhabitants. The wealth of the county's folklore is also inspired by this legacy and Thomas J. Westropp has recorded many of the bountiful myths and legends of Clare. It is perhaps a natural follow-on then that the county has also produced some brilliant writers, poets and scholars such as the soldier poets Hugh MacCurtain and Thomas Dermody, Gaelic poet, Donnchadh Rua MacConnmhara, playwright and critic, Mairéad Ní Gráda, Gaelic author, Micheál Ó Gríofa who drafted the Irish text of *Bunreacht na hÉireann*, the two renowned antiquarians and professors, Eugene O'Curry and Brian Ó Luanaigh right up to today's acclaimed novelist, Edna O'Brien.

We love our music but we love our hurling too. Its 1995 and triumphant Clare captain, Anthony Daly, in the first flush of victory, tells an enraptured audience from the steps of the Hogan Stand in Croke Park about the meas, the respect, with which Clare people hold their culture and traditions. Clare has always had a vibrant traditional music scene and her many gifted and unheralded musicians have preserved and bequeathed to the last and first generations either side of the millennium divide an enlightened respect for Irish culture. They are the living embodiment of the Gaelic legacy, earthy and noble, with both wit and depth, guardians of a heritage. Many commentators and visitors have remarked on the love of learning that prevailed in Clare, even during the numbing times of the penal laws. Pat Mitchell, recalling the jealously guarded manuscripts of poetic compositions that would be fleetingly taken down from the scraws of thatched roofs for consultation, referred to one such manuscript that belonged to the Clancy family in Miltown-Malbay from which sprang the famed piper, Willie Clancy. In it there were references to their kinsman, Conor Óg McClancy, the chief poet of the Thomond bardic school in the 1480s. In this county, there lived poetic dynasties.

You hear the musical names. Éigse Mrs.Crotty and Kilrush, Dan Furey's Labasheeda, Feakle's trad, the céilí bands of Tulla and Kilfenora and Christy Moore's Lisdoonvarna, Garrett Barry's Inagh, Micko Russell's Doolin and Willie Keane's Doonbeg, music, dance and names that echo and beat around the hearths and flagstones and throughout the world. If you hear the music clear enough, you can also hear the wails of deserted homesteads and villages, once populated by Gaelic speakers in their hundreds and in their thousands. On the eve of the visitation of the Great

Famine in 1841, around 286,000 people populated the county. In a devastating ten-year period, almost 50,000 people died of famine and disease. Within forty years the population was halved and almost halved again in the following thirty years. The decline in population continued unchecked for 125 years, reaching its nadir of 73,597 in 1966. From Clare there was an exodus of biblical proportions.

> *Was my mother lonely that Thursday morning? Well I could have cried my eyes red that morning, but for her sake I tried to keep up as best I could. Then the parting at Ennis Station with your father and Frances and P.J. and all the rest. Then in Limerick was just as bad again, as I felt it very hard parting with Kathleen.*
>
> Susan Hegarty, Kilmaley,
> in a letter to her father on her arrival in Rhode Island, USA, 1927.

Between 1851, when reliable recording of emigrant departures began, and 1881, 100,496 Clare women and men left the county, the vast majority never to return. From the pampas of Argentina to the streets of New York, from the bush country of the Australian interior to the docklands of Liverpool, there settled wave after wave of economic refugees in search of hope, if not survival. Their story became part of the story of the seventy million people of the Great Irish Diaspora: abject misery, heroic failure, faith and endurance, survival and triumph. It had always been so, even before the Great Famine of the mid-nineteenth century. Many first generation Clare natives and their descendants dreamed and awoke to realise their destinies. They were in the French vanguard in victorious battles at Fontenoy [1745] and at Ramillies [1706] (seizing the standards of Winston Churchill's kinsman, the Duke of Marlborough – they are still on view today at Kylemore Abbey), they led the storming of the Bastille [1789], they hurled under Kilmurry McMahon's Chevalier O'Gorman in front of King Louis XV and an adoring Parisian public. Even the French mayonnaise was named in honour of the Dalcassian, Marshal Mahon, who took Napoleon's dictum of an army marching on its stomach to heart!

They were deported 'Down Under' as guests of the King, and are honoured for governing territories and discovering the 'Golden Mile' in Kalgoorlie, Australia. They were hunted down for defying tyranny and its excises at Eureka Stockade and were turned to for mediation between nations great and small during the Irish War of Independence. They resisted the Kaiser's son at the River Ourcq and fought communism in the States while Kilkee's Che Guevara Lynch inspired red revolution in the Americas. They have been on the 'beat' on the streets of Chicago and America's eastern cities and 'used their fists for hammers' as they too helped to build the Promised Land and the canals and dams that harnessed it. 'Killaloe' has been belted out as a regimental tune in the South African military for over a century and missionaries have carried with them the zeal of the early Clare Christian, Saint Senan, throughout the economically developing world. They came from the house of the Count of Thomond and led the first European settlement of the Amazon River in 1621, even winning the admiration of the fierce Amazonian women in the process. This is written in the O'Brien Chronicle, a 17th century Old Spanish manuscript in the National Library of Brazil (translated by a Maryland friar, Martin McDonnell) which was prepared as a petition by Captain General Sir Bernard O'Brien del Carpio for the King of Spain. It was also in South America that existed one of the last and largest Clare-Irish speaking areas of the 20th century, near Buenos Aires, Argentina, where the extended Carmody family and neighbours from Clare settled in the 1850s.

Throughout the sporting arenas of the world, the sons and daughters of Clare have stood proud. Keith Wood, Anthony Foley and Marcus Horan have led from the front, the Irish rugby renaissance in the professional era. Clare and Limerick rugby is spiritually entwined. Mick Kennedy, Gary Breen and especially Kevin Sheedy with his cultured ciatóg (leftie) have had accomplished soccer careers. Pat McDonnell, the Doonbeg collossus, won Olympic gold for the U.S in the shot-putt. Fanny Durack has swum to Olympic gold for Australia. Kieran Sheedy, in his book, *The Horse in County Clare*, illustrates the racing tradition here that goes back to the early decades of the 18th century when Sir Edward O'Brien was a renowned owner and breeder, both at Dromoland and Newmarket in England. The first Irish bred horse to win the Aintree Grand National, Matthew in 1847, was bred at Coolreagh, Bodyke. Shannon Lass was another Aintree Grand National champion, bred and trained by the Reidys of Rineanna, where Shannon Airport now stands. Amongst the champion jockeys the county has produced are Tommy Cullinane, Jason Titley and Kieran Fallon. The pride of Kilnamona, Michael Francis McTigue, was the first Irishman to win a world boxing title on Irish soil, defeating Battling Siki for the World Light Heavyweight title before a highly charged crowd in Dublin on St Patrick's Day 1923 at the height of the civil war. Indeed, the first Irish born world boxing champions were the Gardner brothers, George and Jimmy, from Lisdoonvarna. Their father, Pat, no mean bare-knuckle fighter himself, moved his young family to Lowell, Massachusetts, a place which has had close Clare connections for over a century and it was from here that their Celtic fists found glory. And indeed did not the blood of his Dalcassian ancestor O'Grady flow through the veins of the Greatest as he rumbled through the jungle and the last forty years?

To watch or play a game of hurling or football is to take in an experience of the lifeblood of Irish life and Gaelic culture. Clare's emergence as a hurling power in the mid-1990s helped to give the ancient game a higher profile than it ever enjoyed before. These games exude skill, speed, courage and strength and are rooted in antiquity. One of the earliest historical references to the game of hurling in Clare is in a poem written by Lochlainn Ó Dálaigh between 1550 and 1559 in honour of three young hurlers of the O'Brien family of Thomond. It was Michael Cusack from Carron in North Clare, a great visionary, who was the father-founder of the Gaelic Athletic Association in 1884. It was established during the blooming of the 'culture club' throughout Europe as games became codified and organised. They took off, in his words, 'like a prairie fire'. County championships were contested in Clare from 1887 and very keen parish-based club rivalries began. There is a pronounced geographical division of playing codes in the county, and as a general rule of thumb there is an invisible boundary line drawn north of the Fergus estuary through Ennis to the Galway border separating the footballing nations of West Clare from the hurling atistocracies of East Clare, with Eire Óg, Ennis, and a few other clubs, very much a love divided.

The great hurling poet Jimmy Smyth, who holds the scoring record for a Munster championship match, scoring six goals and four points against Limerick in 1953, recalls Ó Riain's ballad, *The Spirit of the Bannermen*:

We are a proud Dalcassian race, who sprang from noble clan,
Steeped deep in lore and legend since records first began.
For music song or dancing, no county can compare
With the spirit of the Bannermen in the storied County Clare

... *"Come on the Banner" in the heat of the fray*
Is the Claremen's clarion call.
In their saffron and blue they are ever true
As they challenge and chase the ball ...

Clare is the Banner County, a moniker, which was garnered from various sources over time. The historian, Ó Dálaigh relates that it was probably arrived at by the custom of greeting politicians with banners, especially popular politicians in Clare like Parnell and de Valera, surviving longer in Clare than in other counties. The

Parnell and de Valera eras coincided with the rise of the GAA and the name soon transferred to the county's hurling and football teams. The banners seized or displayed by Clare's Dragoons at Fontenoy and Ramillies in the 18th century may also have influenced it. The men of Dal gCais carried banners at the Battle of Clontarf and it is said that Boru's banner, the Geal Greine with its thirteen rays of saffron sunburst set against a royal blue backdrop (which was also the flag of the Tuatha De Danann and of the Fianna) inspire the county colours of saffron and blue.

This is but one vision of Clare. The beauty of this county is that any of the over 100,000 people who now call this place home and any of its extended family abroad or any of its many enchanted visitors could paint you a different picture.

Peering down on the streets of Ennis from a Doric column 74 feet high, stands Daniel O'Connell captured in neoclassical pose. He towers above the site of the old courthouse in the main square of Ennis, where the *Liberator* was declared M.P. in 1828 after an overwhelming victory in the famous Clare election, which convinced Wellington and the Peel that Catholic Emancipation could not be delayed. *"You men of Clare have given me an arm powerful enough to strike for justice and to devote my life to my country"* O'Connell told his tenant supporters.

Kieran Sheedy in the Clare Elections recounts how O'Gorman Mahon, a colourful Clare gentleman and duellist (he nominated O'Connell for the seat and stage-managed his election campaign), made the celebrated riposte when requested to remove his sash within the courthouse by the County Sheriff; *"This gentleman tells that gentleman that if that gentleman presumes to touch this gentleman, then this gentleman will defend himself against that gentleman or any other gentleman while he has the arm of a gentleman to protect him"*. The request was withdrawn.

Journeyman blacksmith Martin Kennedy, who used to travel from forges and gatherings, composing and selling broadsheets, penned the following verse for a ballad (sang to the air of the boys of Wexford) in the said Considine's honour:

Ennis men remember, 'twas in your town and square,
O'Connell was selected by those gallant men of Clare,
the galling yoke of our church he broke, and the banner proudly flying,
'Twas grasped by hands like iron bands,
Of bold Mickey Considine.

Initiated by Michael Considine, Ennis, a labour leader, the present monument was erected in 1867. However the historian Ó Murchadha relates that the construction of the statue was not without struggle as Ennis began to feel the pangs of Famine again in the 1861-64 period and its completion took several years as even scaffolding rotted.

Today the monument dominates O'Connell Square (known locally as the Height). Ennis' picturesque narrow streets converge here. Large markets were formerly held and the Square is still very much the focal point of Ennis when crowds gather for homecomings, open-air performances, parades and political hustings.

O'Connell Street, Ennis

Tomás O'Maoldomnaiġ

Steele's Rock

Where the river Fergus, weaving its way through Ennis turns directly towards Clonroad Bridge, there lies close by this bend, an assembly of three odd shaped limestone boulders. The main rock which lies on top of one of two submerged rocks, bears the carving and painting of a shield depicting the figure of a lion raising its left foreleg outwards to the river. It was from this rock that Honest Tom Steele of Cullane House, Clonlea, tormented by an unrequited love, would stand and gaze across the Fergus at Abbeyfield House for a floating glimpse of the mercurial and alluring beauty of Miss Matilda Crowe.

Thomas Ennis Steele was a Protestant landlord and although seeming an unlikely choice for Head Pacificator of Daniel O'Connell's Catholic Association, his integrity, generosity and courage marked him as a man apart. Such was his devotion to O'Connell that in a rather impetuous act, he brought the *Umbilicus Hiberniae*, the stone said to mark the centre of Ireland at Birr, to Cullane where O'Connell often sojourned, for he felt that the centre of Ireland was wherever *The Liberator* went. It was perhaps with this grand larceny in mind that the 'Faithful County' returned the compliment on the hurling fields of 1998. It must be remarked however that the stone was returned to Birr in 1974.

As for Honest Tom Steele, he was also to acquit himself as an inventor of underwater appliances such as a diving bell which he patented and proposed to utilise in blasting dangerous submerged rocks to improve navigation of the Shannon. It was into the waters of the Thames of London he flung himself in 1848, as his friend O'Connell had passed away and the movement for which they both laboured was torn asunder by dissension between the doves of the Repeal Association and the hawks of the Young Ireland movement led by Clareman, William Smith O'Brien. Though rescued, he died a few days later, a ruined man, as the spectre of famine loomed in Ireland.

Abbeyfield, home of the elusive Miss Crowe, was later to house the RIC and then in turn the Garda Síochána and the Fórsa Cosanta Aitiúil, the local defence force.

Tomás Ó Maoldomnaiġ

There was once a strong military tradition in Ennis amongst the old town families, particularly in the service of the British Army during its imperial rule. Sean Spellissy, a renowned local historian, has traced the lineage of US Secretary of Defence, Colin Powell, to one of these families, who had settled in Ennis after the wars of the seventeenth century. The working class of Ennis and of Kilrush particularly suffered while soldiering during the Great War. These men of Ennis are commemorated in a stained glass memorial at St. Columba's Church of Ireland Church, Bindon Street. Ennis was also to become a focal point for revolutionary fervour from the 1860s. There was a massive funeral held for the once exiled Fenian leader Stephen Joseph Meaney in 1888.

In the background stands the Pro-Cathedral of Saints Peter and Paul. Designed by Dominic Madden, it was built on a site donated by Francis Gore, a Protestant landlord whose family were descended from the Cromwellian officer, John Gore, who settled in Clare in 1659 and became one of Ennis' most prominent landholders. Work on it began two years after the Catholic Emancipation Act of 1829 and a dedication ceremony was held in February 1843. The spire and porches were added in 1871.

St. Mary's Church

Another prominent building from the nineteenth century is St. Mary's Franciscan Church. It has been based on its site since 1854, the present having been constructed since 1884 and has continued the presence of Franciscan friars in the town since its foundation.

The *Clare Champion* newspaper offices are located on part of the site of the old Ennis military barracks on a street formerly known as Pump Road. Gallows' Green, once located opposite these barracks is now marked by a car park. As the seat of the county town with vibrant commercial and political activities, it was here in Ennis that legislative decisions, taxes and appeals were made, and officers chosen. It was the only common ground for all sides and factions.

Old Barrack Street and the Pro-Cathedral

SOLICITORS
TWIN BLADES
Tomás Ó Maoldomhnaigh

A feature of the architectural heritage of Clare is the detached, seven bay, three storey, neo-Classical courthouse located on a slight rise on the north bank of the Fergus River in Ennis. There is a degree of confusion amongst historians as to the identity of the designer of the erected building but correspondence from the National Archives may shed some clarity on the matter. It is accepted that John B. Keane drew up the original set of plans for the new Ennis Courthouse in 1838 but, after interest temporarily flagged, a new competition was held in which Henry Whitestone emerged victorious with designs which bore an uncanny resemblance to Keane's previous submission.

It is claimed that this is why Keane and Whitestone are frequently confused as the building's architect. Yet an accessions folder in the National Archives indicates that there may have been a fusion between the two sets of plans. On it is written the following: *Building plans for County Courthouse, Ennis by Henry Whitestone, Architect as adopted by Clare Grand Jury, 25 October 1845 and as erected – found in Store Room,7/6/(19)32.* Yet also associated with the folder is a *'Plan of the second storey for County Courts at Ennis by John B. Keane, Architect'.*

Regardless, this imposing structure with its limestone ashlar façade and ionic portico, still cuts as impressive a sight today as it did when it was described by a newspaper over 150 years ago as *'uncommonly bold and beautiful'.*

As one of the last people to have worked in this building, with Clare's first county curator Dominic Egan, before recent renovation in 1999, I always made a point of saluting Sir Michael O'Loughlen, Master of the Rolls and Attorney general in the Melbourne government of the 1830s, who was a solitary lifelike form in the entrance hall.

A large Russian cannon, a trophy of the Crimean campaign, is situated in front of the building. Its imperialistic connotations aroused the ire of the patriot Michael Considine who led the collection to build another Clare landmark, the O'Connell Monument, which was erected on the site of the old Ennis courthouse.

Ennis Courthouse

The distinctive terraces and rock pavements of the Burren (from the Irish word Boireann – a rocky place) were formed when glaciers plucked layers of stone from the hillsides. The limestone plateau of the Burren was once an ancient seabed and provided a warm, muddy home for marine life. Today, both its smooth and shattered pavements are seedbed habitats for the amazingly diverse array of plants and wildflowers. Here alpine and arctic plants growi side by side with Mediterranean species.

The Gulf Stream, soft rain, relative absence of frost and their carboniferous bedding are among the conditions that contribute to this phenomenon. Brendan Dunford and John Feehan have confirmed in study what many in the Burren have always claimed; that man had lived in harmonious co-existence with the landscape and was an integral part of the Burren eco-system for over six thousand years. It was overgrazing and clearance of the pine dominated woodland with its understory of hazel that exposed so much bare limestone in the first place, the soil washing away down the fissures. However the declining farming traditions of the region have allowed hazel to again expand across the thin dry soil.

Hazel was at one time utilised in the making of baskets, fencing, fodder and fuel, yet is now hardly harvested. Free-ranging goat herds, once kept on farms, browse on hazel and move on without chewing it down. New husbandry practices, with emphasis on access and convenience, are forsaking the traditional upland winterages, a practice which along with goat farming had helped to shape the immense variety of building styles found in the stone architecture of the Burren hills.

All this has accelerated the growth of hazel scrub over the last decade alone which in turn threatens to shade out the flower-rich grassland and swarm over archaeological monuments. Once hazel grows near six foot, only mechanical diggers can clear it which in turn can wreak ecological and archaeological havoc.

You see from this that farmers, often vilified for environmental neglect, have been central to the Burren Circle of Life over the millennia. Perhaps the envisaged integrated environmental management strategy, with incentives for farmers as guardians of a living tradition, will help to maintain the delicate balance between scrub, grassland and heathland areas in the Burren. It may also help to pass on to our following kin, the heritage of the Burren wonderland.

Mullaghmore

Poulnabrone portal tomb is the most famous landmark of the Burren, probably the most photographed monument in the county. Cromwellian general, Ludlow, quoted a saying of the Burren, while pillaging his way through Clare, *'… there is not enough earth to bury a man'.* Well, people had been buried in the Burren for 5000 years before Ludlow's appearance on the Clare landscape in monuments that were ancient before the pyramids at Gisa were even conceived.

This megalithic grave was also probably a site of deep spiritual significance to those who built it. The portal stone of this tomb is aligned towards the rising sun. This is an architectural characteristic of portal tombs whereas the later wedge tombs such as at Gleninsheen are aligned towards the setting sun. One quarter of all the known wedge tombs in the country are situated in Clare. Lying at the centre of the Burren, Poulnabrone dates to the Neolithic period and a series of radio-carbon dates on bones excavated from here go back from 3800BC to 3200BC. It consists of a single chamber with an entrance flanked by two large portal stones and topped with an enormous cap stone that weighs nearly ten tons. The chamber is encased in a very low cairn, which may not have been any higher in antiquity.

The chamber contained the disarticulated bones of twenty one Neolithic men, women and children, as well as cattle, pigs, dogs and sheep/goats. Just outside the entrance a complete skeleton of a new born baby was found. On display at the award winning Riches of Clare exhibition at Clare Museum is the pelvis of an adult male with an embedded tip of a projectile that was discovered in this portal tomb. This wound shows no trace of healing or infection, so the injury would have occurred at the time of death.

Within the vicinity of Poulnabrone is the well preserved stone built ring fort, Cathair Chonaill and a Bronze Age Stone Circle is also located here. Nearby is the newly opened Cathair Chonaill Interpretative Centre. The beautiful Gleninsheen Gold Collar was discovered a little north of here in1932 and is now on display in the National Museum as a national treasure.

Poulnabrone

Tomás O'Maoldomhnaigh

About three hundred yards north of the old church of Gleninagh, near the prominent castle, is a fifteenth century wellhouse, *Tobar na Croiche Naoimh*, dedicated to the Holy Cross. Here Stations of the Cross are performed and votives are left, such as rags which are tied to the twigs of an overhanging elder tree. Such rag offerings as a form of homage were common where there was a 'blessed bush' at the well.

Christianity has assimilated many sites that were once held as sacred in pagan Ireland. Indeed many church celebrations would seem to have their root in the pre-Christian festivals such as *Lughnasa*. This celebration marked the end of summer and the start of the harvest when the first meal of the new crop was usually eaten. The Christian celebrations evolved from these festivals with communities gathering at traditional locations for several days of ceremony that involved an all night vigil of prayers, devotional rounds and subsequent singing, drinking, dancing and horse-racing. Austin Clarke's *The Blackbird of Derrycairn* captures this theme of the Irish pagan world meeting the Christian world in the envisioned meeting of Oisín and Saint Patrick.

Gleninagh (Valley of Ivy), with its once important and ancient village nearly vanished from the north Clare landscape, was one of the last bastions of Clare Irish native speakers. Peadar Ó hAnnracháin wrote of the Irish language of North Clare: '*Is binn an teanga atá ag na sean-daoine ann*' (The language of the old people is sweet). This area was actually a Gaeltacht when the Irish Free State was established.

Outside of Gleninagh, the largest Clare Irish speaking area was near Buenos Aires in Argentina, where the extended Carmody family and friends and neighbours from Clare settled in the 1850s. It remained this community's first language into the 1900s and Clare Irish was known up to the 1930s by which time Spanish had taken over. Tradition has it that it was from Gleninagh pier, not far from the scenic Black Head, that a number of the Wild Geese left this area, and their native homeland, most never to return.

Gleninagh

Tomás O'Maoldomnaig

The impressive promontory of Ceann Boirne is a walker's delight and whether you go solo or in the company of expert local guides, you will experience a magnificent scenery of riveting landscapes, such as the rich pockets of the green Burren grass intermingled with the boney white aura of the rounded limestone hills that fall down to the sea in gentle slopes. Be you a geologist, a botanist, an ornithologist, an archaeologist, a potholer, a Fianna Fáiler, Fine Gaeler or left-winger, or just simply a walker, this is blissful country.

The elevated green roads that are now part of the Burren Way were once part of the ancient northern route from Fanore. Cathair Dhuin Irghuis overlooking Galway Bay on Black Head is a cashel that could be of prehistoric or even medieval date, with the construction of its structural joints indicating different work crews engaged in various sections of the wall. At the summit of Black Head (Gleninagh Mountain) lies the Carn Dobhach Bhrainin, while nearby at the almost levelled Carn Suí Finn, Fionn MacCumhaill defeated the folkloric intruder, Lonn MacLeefa. The automated lighthouse at the foot of Black Head is opposite Spiddle, which is lying northwards across the Bay.

The shelves of limestone coastal rock platforms around Black Head are superb natural areas for shore angling. The sand and mud flats along the Bay towards Ballyvaughan provide extensive resting places for migrating seabirds. Further inland and open to the public is Aillwee Cave, said to be two million years old, which features an underground river and waterfall. Aillwee in conjunction with Poulnagollum, the principal cave system in Ireland with over seven and a quarter miles of surveyed passage ways, and Pól an Ionainn in Doolin, one of the world's largest stalactites, all combine to make the Burren a speleologist's heaven.

Continuing eastwards to just outside Ballyvaughan, one can experience a comprehensive audiovisual display on the geology, archaeology and natural history of the Burren at the 'Burren Exposure', just in case the hiking boots can't be located.

Black Head

Tomás Ó Maoldoṁnaiġ

Kilfenora

The picturesque and rejuvenated village of Kilfenora, one of the important gateways to the Burren lying on the south-west border, is the Pope's own diocese. It is on its way towards reclaiming its former glory, with the population decline now arrested and reversed. The formation of a local guild of *Muintir na Tíre*, and the role of *Comhar Conradh na Boirne* here has spearheaded this renaissance. The pioneering Burren Centre, with its new exhibition *'A Journey through Time'* lies in the heart of the village. It presents the story of the Burren from the time when it lay beneath a warm tropical sea to its archaeological landscape today.

St. Fachtnan was said to have founded a church here in the 6th century. However it was when the synod of Rathbreasail snubbed the claims for diocesan status by Kilfenora in 1111 that the O'Connors and the O'Loughlens came together. It was their desire to remain aloof of the diocese of Killaloe which was very much under the patronage of the O'Briens. It was the O'Briens who had burned Kilfenora Abbey and its inhabitants in 1055.

In a show of determination to press its claims, some of the finest stonework bequeathed to us from the period was produced. Seven carved stone crosses are associated with Kilfenora from this era, all survive with one removed to St. Flannan's Cathedral in Killaloe.

The Burren actually had more churches per parish in the thirteenth to sixteenth centuries than anywhere else in Ireland. Some of its medieval churches were decorated by a fine school of twelfth century sculptors specialising in stylised human heads. Kilfenora Cathedral was a focal point, with its present structure dating from the late twelfth century. At the Synod of Kells in 1152 Kilfenora did indeed prevail and win diocesan status and the beautiful Doorty Cross would seem to commemorate this event. However with the limited resources of just thirteen parishes it could not sustain its achievement and is now under the administration of the Galway Catholic diocese with the Pope as its nominal Bishop. Part of Kilfenora Cathedral is still in use for divine worship by the Church of Ireland.

Leamaneh Castle

Standing sentinel at the junction of the Ballyvaughan, Corofin and Kilfenora roads is the ruined fifteenth century castle and seventeenth century manor house of Leamaneh. The appendage of the latter to the original tower house makes the building unique. It takes its name from leim an eich, 'the horse's leap', or leim an fheidh, 'the deer's leap'. The latter may refer to its surviving seventeenth century walled deer park that also enclosed a fish-pond. It was the home of that branch of the O'Brien's from which the Barons Inchiquins of Dromoland Castle claim their descent. Even today, it makes for an imposing presence and one can imagine the pluck it took for the Burren natives to force the castle gates, with which Conor O'Brien controlled immediate approaches to and from the Burren in the 1740s, and guarantee their right of way forever.

It is Conor O'Brien's wife, the famous chatelaine, Maire Rua O'Brien, and the history and myths associated with her, which capture the imagination. She was said to have had strong nymphomaniac tendencies, such as taking on twelve lovers during the absence of her husband Conor. Some tales have her marrying twenty five times while continuing to annex new properties. Another story claims that in giving vent to her jealous impulses she would hang her maids from the castle by their hair or cut their breasts off.

Dromoland Castle

What history can assuredly verify were her survival instincts. Westropp recounts that, during the Cromwellian wars, her husband was carried mortally wounded back to Leamaneh. She held onto him as he passed away to the next life and upon this, she immediately set off for Limerick, which was besieged by Ireton, Cromwell's son-in-law and leader of the army that slew her husband. Encountering the Cromwellians, she cried 'I was Conor O'Brien's wife yesterday and his widow today' and to confirm Conor's death, Captain Cooper took her for his bride. In doing so, the O'Brien property was saved for her son Donough. He was to transfer the family residence to Dromoland Castle in 1685-86. Thus ended the pattern of continuous settlement at this strategic site which dated from the Cathair Scribin ring fort c. 400 A.D.

Doonagore Castle, Doolin

About midway between the Cliffs of Moher and the famed musical fishing village of Doolin stands the castle of Doonagore. It overlooks Inis Oirr and Crab Island, the latter carving its niche in Irish history as being the place from where the stranded Sergeant Dowling, carrying the 'Kaiser's gold', was picked up and detained by the coastguard authority in 1918. Having been identified as a leading conspirator in a so called German Plot, it presented the authorities with the opportunity to crack down on the rising republican movement in both Clare and Ireland as a whole at a time when the threat of conscription loomed large.

Doonagore Castle displays physical characteristics that seem straight from a fairytale pop-up book or perhaps a Gaudi vision. It was recently restored under the private ownership of the O'Gormans in the 1970's. The O'Connor clan had held this district from antiquity down to 1582, and it was Teigue MacTurlough MacCon O'Connor who founded Doonagore Castle, around the fourteenth century. It takes its name from the now levelled Dun na nGabhar, or Fort of the Goats. Doonagore is one of the three round castles which stand in Clare. The other two are Newtown in Ballyvaughan and Faunarooska and they, along with Doonagore, all lie in the north east of Clare, the historic Corcomroe region.

Within the shadow of Doonagore is an Iron Age ring barrow burial mound. Some of the primitive tools found in the Doolin area close by over a century ago, such as stone choppers, hand axes and flakes, all indicate that the Mesolithic people, Ireland's earliest recorded inhabitants, were present in the area around 8,000 years ago. Much later activity included quarrying, which was crucial to the local economy around this part of Clare, and Doonagore flagstone was central to this industry. These flagstone slabs, with the distinctive fossilised patterns were in much demand and were used to pave the Royal Mint in London.

It is amongst the public houses of Doolin and Roadford that the heartbeat of traditional Irish music is best felt, and the legendary Russell brothers – Micho, Pakie and Gus, who are commemorated in a visitor centre here, were foremost amongst those that helped to keep this flame burning from the 1950s onwards.

Tomás O'Maoldoṁnaiġ

Probably the defining landmark of Clare, the Cliffs of Moher are the county's most famous tourist spot with their great bands of shale and sandstone rising 660 feet above the Atlantic waves. These giant natural ramparts extend from Hags Head to Aill na Searrach, a stretch of five miles across Clare's coastline, to form the Great Wall of Thomond. The cliffs take their name from Mothair Uí Ruis, or Ruain, a promontory fort that was once located on Hag's Head, where one may now see the ruins of a tower from the Napoleonic era.

Folklore relates how the hag, Mal, pursued Cuchulainn to Loop Head and jumped after him to Diarmuid and Grainne's Rock. Springing back to the mainland, she was dashed to pieces, reddening the sea with her blood as far as Moher and thus giving the name Malbay to nearby Miltown. It is the sheer vertical scale of the cliffs that make them so daunting.

Cornelius O'Brien was a local landlord from Birchfield House near Liscannor who, as the saying goes, 'built everything around here except the Cliffs of Moher'. Some unflattering accounts claim this included building the nearby O'Brien Monument, across from St. Brigid's Well, as a tribute to himself!

O'Brien did however grasp the concept of the value of a local tourist economy, one of the first to do so, and with this in mind he built the gothic tower structure named after him in 1835, on one of the most elevated points of the Cliffs. From this exceptional vantage point a panoramic view of the Irish coastline unfurls, from the Kerry mountains to Connemara.

O'Brien's Tower now accommodates over 650,000 visitors a year. Scenic boat tours of the waters around the Cliffs are now led by families who are descended from generations of fishermen from Liscannor, Doolin and the Aran Islands that have fished here for centuries. Here you are close to the vast colonies of seabirds that inhabit Moher, including guillemots, puffins, razorbills, seagulls, shags and kittiwakes.

Cliffs of Moher

Tomás Ó Maoldoṁnaiġ

There is much here in this bustling market town, two miles from the coastal resort of Lahinch, to recommend itself to the visitor. Ennistymon is famous for its vernacular shop fronts, giving the street façade a distinctive, colourful, character. They are an integral feature of Irish provincial town architecture and a legacy of the indigenous industrial and commercial heritage of the area. The former Market House is a further testament to an era when the town and its substantial hinterland grew prosperous with the coming of the West Clare Railway.

Ennistymon grew as a settlement around the most accessible fording point of the Inagh River which is formed by the joining of the Cullenagh and Derry rivers at a short distance from the idyllic falls. Historians differ as to the origin of its name *Inis Diamain.* Westropp referred to it as the fruitful riverside meadow, Dineen thought it to mean the hidden island but others claim that it came simply from the Anglicisation of *Inis-tigh-mean*, or the house of the middle island. This last explanation refers to the mound where the Falls Hotel now stands and which formerly was an island.

The hotel was previously known as Ennistymon House. Its Georgian portion was built on the ruins of an O'Brien castle in 1764, with a west wing added by the MacNamara family in the 1800s to house the shooting and fishing guests of the 'Lord of the Manor'. The estate covered 18,000 acres and much of the town, and the fortunes of Ennistymon were controlled from this building for over three centuries. Local folklore had it that on the night of 11 December 1876, a servant of the MacNamaras from Ennistymon House, while going his rounds by the tranquil wooded glen bordering the cascading Cullenagh, heard the rumbling of the wheels of 'no mortal vehicle' – the death coach. He had just time to throw himself on his face by the gate he had just opened as the coach did not stop at the house but passed on, and the sound died away. On the following day Admiral Sir Burton MacNamara died in London.

Ennistymon

Tomás O'Maoldomhnaigh

Lahinch

It is the Atlantic surf and golfing turf of the 'Half Island', or Leath Inis, of Lahinch, that have led to its acclaim as a golden jewel of Clare. This famed and ever popular coastal resort was once under the aegis of the O'Connor chieftains of Corcomroe, a period from which the town derives its official Irish name of Leacht Uí Chonchubair, or O'Connor's Cairn. Samuel Lewis describes it in the nineteenth century as having a *'fine bathing strand, situated at the inner extremity of the* [Liscannor] *bay and much resorted to during the season'.*

Probably the two defining events of Lahinch's development came to pass almost within a year of each other in the 1890s. In July of 1893, Lady Aberdeen, wife of the Irish Viceroy, officially opened the newly constructed sea wall and promenade, which faces out on to the mile long sandy beach. This facilitated the exploding number of visitors arriving at Lahinch, especially since the advent of the West Clare railway in 1887. Garland Sunday, which probably originated from the pagan festival *Domhnach Chrom Dubh*, celebrated by the people on the last Sunday of July was a particularly popular occasion when, as Archdeacon James Kenny described in 1775, *'a number of people assemble at Lahinchy: they amuse themselves with horse-racing on the strand, dancing, &c... to conclude their merriment'.*

Earlier, on Good Friday 1892, the mighty golfing challenge that is Lahinch's championship Golf Course was inaugurated, having been established by touring officers of the Scottish Black Watch regiment stationed in Limerick. One of the great champions of what is Ireland's oldest golf championship, the South of Ireland, was John Burke. In the 'South' of 1920 during the fight for independence, he became embroiled in controversy as he and two companions twice raised the tricolour from the club flagstaff. Arriving British military torched the first flag, and the second Tricolour was unceremoniously chopped down along with the flagstaff. Indeed following the nearby Rineen ambush, many buildings in Lahinch were burned down, as the freedom struggle intensified.

Tomás O'Maoldomnaiġ

The Traditional Sessions

Traditional music has always played a powerful role in the life of Clare people. It represents continuity with the past, from wakes and weddings in houses and pubs to gatherings at dances, festivals and sessions. If in the sporting passions of the Banner County you glimpse the heart of Clare, it is at these musical gatherings you see into its soul.

Many tunes have been bequeathed from generations past and were rarely written down, much akin to the béaloideas, or the oral folklore tradition. A number of the composed ballads, although not critical masterpieces nor were they intended as such, are communicative works, works for communal consumption, a public language that reflects the ways of life associated with place and tradition.

The voice, a remarkable musical instrument in itself is used to embellish the richness of song and stories in Clare along with the fiddle, whistle, flute, uileann pipes and concertina. A host of individual masters and the famous Kilfenora and Tulla céilí bands have carved a niche in the musical world and have made it their own. Glór, the newly opened major cultural centre in Ennis, celebrates the renowned master musicians of Clare.

Dance is another form of expression, a movement of emotion, as once commonly seen at the crossroads like in Ballyea and at popular céilí such as in Corofin. Labasheeda's Dan Furey was an expert practitioner of this art and this tradition has been continued on by dancing talents such as James Devine from Ardnacrusha, who holds a Guinness world record for step dancing, beating out thirty eight taps in a second.

Clare is a by-word for rich traditional music and this scene here at Miltown Malbay, the west Clare home of Gaelic musicians and poets such as Micheal Ó Coimín, Tomas Ó hAodha and Willie Clancy, is the archetypal county setting.

Tomás Ó Maoldomhnaigh

From the Hand to the Clogher, from Doolough Lake to Clohauninchy, there lives a community binded by tradition. A generosity of spirit and sincerity are the defining traits of these people, a personality that has been shaped by the sea. For by living off the sea and 'ploughing the ocean' since antiquity, a spirit of interdependence and camaraderie has been engendered amongst the fishing folk of Quilty and its surrounds. They have harvested sea vegetables such as *sleabhacán* and Carrageen and gathered seaweed, which was burned in kilns to make kelp which yielded iodine. The seaweed was gathered from the shore at the time of the May *giorradh*, or stirring of the tide which indicated that the seaweed was ripe and breaking off.

Many a ship has been driven from the stormy ocean onto the jagged reefs here. Amongst these has been a 'Big Ship' from the Spanish Armada fleet which was wrecked off the reef between Mutton Island, or Inis Caorach, and the mainland, and swept by the prevailing current from here to Spanish Point.

The cry of 'Viva la Quilty' heard throughout France and Ireland in October 1907 was inspired by the heroics of the thirty-one intrepid Quilty fishermen who braved the treacherous weather conditions in their sturdy curraghs, and rescued the majority of the crew of the stricken French ship, *Leon XIII.* Their courage and their faith helped to provide the village of Quilty with the Star of the Sea Church, as a fund for a new church was opened to commemorate the deeds of the fishermen. They were also paraded down O'Connell St., Dublin, with their faithful curraghs, to the acclaim of thousands.

One of the notable reefs that jut out from Tromoroe is Carraiganuala. It is associated with the mythical woman Fionnuala who pursued her lover to this reef, which was the last outpost before the Atlantic. Here the tale turns gruesome as the man disembowelled Fionnuala and her remains were washed up on the neighbouring reef, Carraig an Putóg, or the rock of the pudding, which also takes its name from this episode. The third reef in this vicinity, Carraig an Bheidhlin, is so named because of its violin shape and alludes to the strong musical tradition here.

Kilmurry Ibrickane

Kilkee and the Scenic Loop Coastline

Clare is known as a county of seascapes and landscapes, and Kilkee's crescent shaped beach is one of its premier coastal resorts. The coastal drive around Carmel and the Big Sur in California is much lauded but if it is half as magnificent as the scenic route between Kilkee and the Loop Head peninsula, then it truly deserves its accolades.

Beginning from the West End of Kilkee, one arrives at the natural barrier of the Duggerna Rocks where marine life abounds in the rock pools. Here is similar to on up the coast at Loch Donnell, between Doughmore and Kilmurry Ibrickane, where in the abundant rock pools the only fish in the sea with a trade, the cobbler fish or donnán, can be caught by using a small hook baited with the meat of the barnach that cling to the reef.

Continuing on past the Amphitheatre, with its tiers of seat-like rocks that has hosted outdoor concerts, the Pink Cave, Lion Head Rock and the Diamond Rocks, you come to Intrinsic Bay, named after the ship that was wrecked here in 1836, and Look-Out Hill, from where there are wonderful vistas of the Irish coastline.

The Bridge of Ross

Further on, the curious ruins at Bishop Island (although it appears to look like a stack) always attract interest, standing as it does like a blasted, defiant force against the Atlantic. These are held by many to be the remains of Saint Senan's Oratory, the much venerated Saint in West Clare who was said to have erected this little oratory before finally settling at Inis Cathaigh, or Scattery Island after defeating the sea monster, Cathach. However the renowned Gaelic scholar Eugene O' Curry who hailed from nearby Doonaha claimed there was no local tradition to link Senan with Bishop Island.

Taking this route to access Kilbaha on the seventeen mile Loop Head peninsula, you pass the ruins of the fifteenth century McMahon stronghold, Dunlicky Castle and turn inland at Goleen Bay through Newtown and travel four miles by the main road to the friendly village of Cross. A couple of miles beyond here are one of nature's classics, the Bridge of Ross. A natural landform, this sea-arch highlights the exposed bedded and folded rock of coastal Clare.

Tomás O'Maoldoṁnaiġ

West Clare was once the ancient territory of Corca Bhaiscinn. Inhabited by the Fir Bolg, it came under the influence of the Milesians around the third century A.D. and it was from this stock that the Patron of West Clare, St. Senan came. The land here has had its jousts with both the sea and the Shannon Estuary.

It is written in the Annuals of the Four Masters that in 799A.D. *'A great storm of wind, thunder and lightening happened this day before St. Patrick's festival this year, and it killed ten and one thousand persons in the Territory of Corca Baiscinn, and the Sea divided the island of Inis Fithae into three parts.'*

There are constant references throughout the ages to the mystical land of Kilstephen, which is said to have been submerged at this time. The event of Senan's expulsion of the Monster Cathach from the ancient diocese of Scattery Island to Doolough Lake which is by the southern slope of Mount Callan, has lent itself to association with places such as Gleann na Péiste, Valley of the Serpent, where St. Senan's Well is located outside Kilrush, and the snaking valley at Clonreddan in the Cooraclare and Cree heartlands. There is today in Kilrush, the capital of west Clare, a heritage trail from the Vandeleur Walled Gardens to Kilrush Creek and Marina, the Scattery Island Heritage Centre and the old West Clare Railway station. Kilrush was the terminus of the old railway and also the destination for river steamers from Limerick carrying many seaside-bound visitors.

The West Clare Railway, immortalised in song by Percy French, and its distinctive narrow gauge, cut fifty-three miles of track through the west like a pair of lungs. It acted as an outlet to the outside world for over seventy years. One travel writer wrote that *'locals used to come to the crowded little platforms just to meet the train'*. It also helped to service the local industries. With its regretful closure in 1961, it passed into the heritage of the region. Indeed a group of dedicated locals have recently restored part of the original line at Moyasta junction and it is a popular attraction in the west.

West Clare and the Railway

Maġ Ṡeasta
MOYASTA

Clondegad Falls and the hidden beauty of Clare

Within the many and varied regions of Clare are areas of distinctive beauty, enhanced by their hidden, secluded nature. Not often marked on tourist trails, they possess a capacity to surprise and delight, and it is here amongst these places and people that the true Banner unfurls.

It may be in the Kildysart of O'Connell Bianconi, where you can go from the wood sheltered mass rock of Ballylean to the bustling local village where the Irish patriot Peadar Clancy of nearby Cranny is commemorated in the main square and the tragic Colleen Bawn is buried, or further south along the widening Shannon at the traditional fishing village of Labasheeda.

It could be somewhere along the quintessential Irish route from Ballynacally through Lack, Cranny, The Six Crosses in Kilmurry McMahon and Knockerra to Kilrush, part of the ancient borderlands of Thomond, east and west. Perhaps you find secreted gems at the Millennium Park by Doolough Lake, the Glennagallaigh Pass in Broadford or at the idyllic boating village of Mountshannon, straddling Lough Derg, Ireland's pleasure lake. It could be in O'Curry's country in Carrigaholt.

The melodious cascading falls on the Clondegad River, near to the parish divide between all things Lissycasey and all things Ballynacally, encapsulate such beauty. Not far from where the river empties into the Fergus are stunning hillside views of the island spangled confluence of the Shannon and Fergus estuaries, where Inishmore, Coney Island, Canon Island, Horse Island, Corcory Island, Feenish and Deenish islands and Inishmacnaghtan, were once areas of ecclesiastical and agricultural importance. Indeed, the rich mudflats or slob lands of the Fergus around Islandavanna were reclaimed over a century ago due to the inspiration of the aptly named, H.G. Drinkwater, a conscientious Manchester entrepreneur.

You can walk the pilgrim's path between the old Rocky Road in Ennis and Killone Abbey, lunch off Lake Inchiquin at Corofin or sup the black stuff at traditional sessions in Walshes in Cree.

These are but little cameos of the hidden Clare, the living Clare.

Before the Battles of Kilbarron and Dysert O'Dea had expelled the Normans from Clare, they had set about erecting castles or strongholds in their newly acquired territory. Robert de Muscegros was granted the lands of Tradaree in South Clare as part of the Anglo Norman policy of conquest and settlement.

At Bunratty (or Bun Ráite, the mouth of passages, a reference to the Owenogarney River that runs through this site) he erected the first fortress here around 1251. Muscegros received permission to cut down oak trees at Cratloe to construct castles and palisades here and at Clarecastle and thus began a pattern of the denudation of the great forests of East Clare for military purposes, a trend that continued right up to the building of the Hearts of Oak war ships that won fame at the Battles of the Nile and Trafalgar. So densely wooded was the East Clare region that local tradition reckoned a squirrel could travel from Lough Graney to Clooney and from Killaloe to Cratloe and never touch the ground.

The history of Bunratty castle very much mirrored the fortunes of the Normans in this county. The fortifications and lands of Muscegros passed to another Norman Knight, Lord Thomas de Clare in 1276 and many of his followers settled throughout Tradaree. It remained a de Clare stronghold for the next forty years. The de Clares became entangled in a bitter O'Brien feud over succession to the Munster kingship, supporting Brian Rua O'Brien's claims, but following upon the alliance's defeat at Magh Gressa, Brian Rua was turned on by his erstwhile allies and was savagely torn apart by horses at Bunratty castle.

Shortly after the de Clares suffered a crushing defeat at Dysert O'Dea. When news of the deaths of her husband and son came to de Clare's wife, she took stock of the situation and promptly burned the castle and town before fleeing for England.

A new chapter began at Bunratty when Síoda McNamara built the present castle in the fifteenth century. Contemporary scenes from this time are today re-enacted here and famous medieval banquets are held in the restored Bunratty Castle and Folk Park, one of Ireland's major tourist attractions.

Bunratty Castle

O'Briens Bridge and Bridgetown

O'Brien's Bridge is a picturesque village on the west bank of the Shannon. It derives its name from the ancient bridge, originally built in 1506 by Turlough O'Brien, first Earl of Thomond and Baron Inchiquin, which crosses the river to what, is now Montpelier in Limerick. Known in antiquity as *Áth Caille Geallaigh*, or The Rough Ford of the Wood, O'Brien's Bridge was once one of the three principal fords of Ireland together with *Áth Cliath* (Dublin) and *Áth Luain* (Athlone).

It was also the site of O'Briens Castle, but it, just like the bridges previous to the present twelve arched one, was destroyed over the ages as the strategically located village, lying midway between Lough Derg and Limerick City, was hotly contested by warring parties. The bridge today came into being following the destruction of the 'Great Bridge', which was defended by marble castles built at each end of the structure. It was destroyed in an attack by Lord Deputy Leonard Gray on the O'Briens who had sided with Silken Thomas in a rebellion against Henry VIII. An interesting feature in the middle of this village today is the Watertree, an apparently resurrected tree from which water is constantly flowing into a small circular pond!

Bridgetown

In the village of Bridgetown close by one can trace Sarsfield's Ride, the route the valiant Jacobite general took when setting about destroying the ammunition train at Ballyneety on its way to Williamites at the besieged city of Limerick. Just south of here is Clonlara, where the striking Falls of Doonass can be seen, although the water has been reduced since the Shannon Hydroelectric scheme, the pioneering rural electrification project, was undertaken by the fledgling Irish Free State at Ardnacrusha in 1925. Also in the vicinity are Meelick, Cratloe and Parteen, areas where the East Clare Brigade under General Michael Brennan were active during the War of Independence.

Tomás O'Maoldoṁnaiġ

Lying at the southern end of Lough Derg on the Shannon River, Killaloe, a designated Heritage Town connected with the Tipperary village of Ballina by a bridge of thirteen arches, is at the heart of an ancient and beautiful district. Brian Boru reigned over the Kingdom of Ireland from here, at the site of Royal Palace of Kincora where the present Roman Catholic Church lies today. It was under the patronage of the Dalcassian Kings that Killaloe became an important centre of Irish religious life.

Donal Mór O'Brien, that great patron of Killaloe diocese, built the Romanesque Cathedral here in 1182, on the site of the first monastery founded by St. Molua, the saint after whom the town is named.

Within a few years the army of Connaught ransacked the Cathedral. It was replaced in the thirteenth century by the present St. Flannan's Cathedral. The Romanesque west doorway of the original Cathedral, one of the finest examples of this style of church architecture in Ireland, was incorporated into the south wall of the new building. On display within the Cathedral today is a shaft of a cross from 1000A.D. bearing an inscription in Scandinavian Runic and Irish Ogham, a unique artefact. The runic inscription reads *'Thorgrimr carved this Cross'*, and the ogham inscription reads *'a blessing upon Thorgrimr'*.

Ogham Stone and Roman Arch

Overlooking the great earthen ring fort of Béal Boru, just outside the town towards Scariff on the western shore of Lough Derg, is Carraig Aoibheal, a great rock, forty feet high. Emerging from the northern side of Crag Liath, it is the legendary habitation of the Banshee of the Dal gCáis, Aoibheal, meaning the 'Lovely One'. It was from here in 1014 that Aoibheal hastened to the Dalcassian camp on the eve of battle against the Dublin Vikings at Clontarf and appeared to Brian Boru, foretelling his death the following day.

Nestling between the Sliabh Bernagh and Sliabh Aughty mountains in the east of Clare, Tuamgraney, or Tuaim Gréine, which refers to either the mount of the sun or the tomb of Grían, is steeped in antiquity. It is part of the ancient territory of Uí Dhonghaile, which incorporated neighbouring Scariff (Moynoe), Tuamgraney, Inis Cealtra (Holy Island) and Clonrush. Its geographic location by Lough Derg, described vividly by an old colleague, MacConmara, as the motorway of ancient Ireland, has bequeathed to it a rich ecclesiastical and historical legacy, and makes it an attractive location on the Lough Derg Way.

The interpretation of Tuaim Gréine as deriving from the tomb of Grían comes from both ancient manuscripts and folklore memory. Grían famed for her beauty, was the daughter of a King from the Sliabh Aughty mountains. Upon discovering her unnatural origin, begotten by a human being on a sunbeam, she determined upon self-destruction and drowned herself in Loch na Bo Girre (now Lough Graney). Her body was carried by stream to Doire Greíne, Derrygraney, where it was found by friends, who interred the remains at what is now the southwest of Tuamgraney village and raised over it a tumulus from which, it is held, Tuamgraney received its name.

The local historian Madden, who provides boat tours of nearby Holy Island, or Inis Cealtra, in Lough Derg, has traced that Tuamgraney is mentioned thirty two times in the ancient Annals. The area certainly abounds with vestiges of the past, be it St. Cronan's Church (whose little doorway is in the same condition as when Brian Boru walked under it), the famine memorial park, the O'Grady castle which was built by that clan to command the ford (from which nearby Scariff or Scarbh, meaning the rocky ford takes its name) or the Calvary of East Clare erected near the Rock of Tuamgraney to commemorate those who fell in the fight for independence between 1916 and 1921. Even nature has chipped in, with the majestic Boru millennium oak tree, holding court close by the village.

Tuamgraney

Tomás Ó Maoldoṁnaiġ

Ballycrom Hill - Merriman's Country

The Gaelic poet Merriman's *Cúirt an Mean Oíche,* or *The Midnight Court,* is a defining work of the late eighteenth century. The countryside around Lough Graney where he lived, wandered and taught, which he knew and loved, remains very much as it was. A hike through the East Clare Way between Feakle and Caher brings you to his country, his inspiration. It was a privilege to go through this countryside in the company of the geologist, Paddy Maher and artist, Tomas O'Maoldomhnaigh.

For Maher, this area is one of the most distinct and unique in the country containing, as it does on Ballycrom Hill, the fascinating geological feature known as an unconformity. In essence, this landmark feature is a time gap which marks the collision of continents, the boundary marking the passing of 30 million or more of the earth's years and the transformation of deep ocean into a desert. You can place your hand on this phenomenon of living natural history, at the juncture between the Silurian vertical, dark grey shales in the lower part of the outcrop and the Devonian horizontal, reddish conglomerated or pebbly sandstone in the upper part.

Continuing this way over the East Clare hills that look out onto Lough Graney, you come to an ancient tomb, which as it gathered bog water over time became known as the Tobergrania dolmen-well. Westropp remarked that the scoop at the west end of the well was where St. Grania put in his head to drink.

Nearby is Altóir Ultach, once the tomb of a Gaelic chieftain, but now better known as a Mass Rock. A megalithic monument, it was constructed of the red pebbly sandstone so prominent here. From these hills and wilds one descends onto Lough Graney where Merriman is commemorated in stone. The East Clare countryside is internationally renowned for its many lakes and is very popular with anglers.

Tomás O'Maoldomnaiġ

Quin and the Abbeys of Clare

As part of their policy of erecting defensive fortifications in newly annexed territories, the Normans under Richard de Clare built Quin Castle in 1280. This, it was envisaged, would subdue the McNamaras of the Clan Cuilein but within six years Cuvea McNamara had sacked the castle and put it to the torch. In one of the quirks of history, the MacNamaras, especially the Síoda MacNamaras, were to become renowned as great castle builders, thus reinforcing their powerful standing in Clare.

The remaining Castle walls were incorporated into the beautiful Romanesque structure that was Quin Abbey. It was founded by the MacNamaras around 1350 and built by the legendary Gobán Saor. Pope Eugenius IV in a Papal Bull to Mahon McNamara sanctioned the foundation of a Franciscan Order here. The Abbey was to have a long history of suppression and violence. The English converted Quin Abbey into a military barracks and placed a garrison here during the Elizabethan suppression of monasteries. Donough Beag O'Brien was put to the death here in much the same way the Scottish legend Braveheart was executed, only in this case O'Brien's mangled body was tied to the steeple of the Abbey as a warning to the locals. The Abbey was sacked again by Cromwellian military and some friars were murdered. The last friar of Quin, Father John Hogan died in 1818, and Quin Abbey became a national monument in the late nineteenth century.

Killone Abbey

Killone Abbey, a convent for Augustinian nuns, now also a National Monument, is located in a setting of great tranquillity beside Killone Lake, rich woodlands and open pasture. Donal Mór O'Brien, King of Thomond introduced the Augustinian Order into Clare towards the end of the twelfth century, granting substantial tracts of land to this monastic order, such as at Clare Abbey and Killone, Inchicronan and at Canon Island in the Fergus Estuary. This was done *'in fear of the many sins he had committed and for the salvation of his soul and the souls of his ancestors and successors'.* Such prolific patronage also had the effect of increasing the O'Brien powerbase, with many of the family becoming bishops of the Killaloe diocese.

God and politics went hand in hand in medieval Ireland.

But when my vision faded, the tears came in my eyes
I hope to see that dear old spot some day before I die
May the Almighty King of Angels His Choicest blessing spill.
On that glorious spot of nature The Cross of Spancilhill.

The bittersweet final verse of Michael Considine's famous 'Spancilhill' as perpetuated by Robbie McMahon in song captures the trauma of separation from home and love.

The words of Spancilhill are engrained in the folk memory of Clare people. Michael Considine emigrated to Boston in 1870. It had been his intention to save sufficient money to enable him to marry his childhood sweetheart Mary McNamara. However things did not pan out that way as a combination of illness and hard work both in Boston and later in California took their toll on him. On realising that he hadn't long to live he decided to send a poem he had written, home to Clare to his young nephew, John, whose father Pat Considine had just died. Michael soon after died. Mary 'Mack', remained faithful to his memory and never married. Young John Considine grew to read the words and they soon became immortalised in song.

Spancilhill, which lies a few miles outside Ennis on the main Ennis-Scariff road, hosts an annual horse fair on 23rd June. It was once one of the greatest of Ireland's fairs. Fairs such as this were communal occasions, beyond buying and selling. Gossip was swapped, friends and foes did greet or voice grievances here and alcohol could occasionally fuel flames of aggression. Not only were cattle, sheep and horses traded at fairs, but matches were made, labourers and tradesmen were hired and carts were bought and sold. The fairs held at places like Sixmilebridge, Tulla and Kilkishen were where the roads converged. Sonny Enright, a cattle dealer, has written of cattle drovers sleeping at night on the 'Widow Green' or the ditch, as they went to and from fairs.

Spancilhill

spancilhill inn
Tomás O'Maoldomhnaigh

The Famine Village and the little Ark of Kilbaha

There are few such visual testimonies to the Great Famine in Clare and Ireland as the poignant sight of the dead villages, such as seen opposite in Drumeen in Tubber or in Caher Bheannach in Fermoyle East. These deserted ruined villages were once were homes to many of the 286,000 people that lived in the county in 1841. About half of all the houses in Clare at this time were one roomed cottages, this along with thousands of destitute squatters, most of whom lived by the sea.

The vast majority of this populace depended upon the potato as a stable food. When the potato blight struck with the rains of August 1845, it set into motion a chain effect of disastrous proportions. The bulk of the people survived the first year of famine but Clare historian Dr Joe Power relates the shocking scenes by the early weeks of Black '47, when the potato crop had been decimated for the second consecutive year:

The Little Ark of Kilbaha

Innocent people starve, especially the women and children, crowds of whom were scattered over the turnip fields like famished crows, devouring the raw turnips: mothers half naked shivering in the snow and sleet uttering exclamations of despair, while their children were screaming with hunger.

Over 40,000 from Clare died in the workhouses alone, due to the effects of starvation and disease, and another 40,000 emigrated during this apocalypse.

In the church at Moneen, in Kilbaha on the Loop Head peninsula, there stands preserved the Little Ark. From the past's foreign country, the Little Ark now resides in the third millennium, and it tells both visitors and the local descendants of Kilbaha's churchless, post-famine people, of a time of struggle between the landed Messrs. Burton and Westby and their agent Marcus Keane and Father Michael Meehan, parish priest of Carrigaholt, and his congregation. It resulted in the Mass being said from this humble wooden box, supported on four wheels, on the strand in Kilbaha between 1852 and 1857 when a site was eventually secured for a church.

Tomás Ó Maoldomhnaigh

The famed parish of Dysert O'Dea holds within it a treasure chest of archaeological and historical wealth which spans the millennia. It has the Roman like virtue of simulating one great outdoor museum. Here you can stroll through the ages, exploring Holy wells, ancient high crosses and burial grounds (cillín), soup schools, hedge schools, limekilns and 'Big Houses' as well as round towers, abbeys, ancient roadways, earthen forts, stone forts and castles both ruined and restored.

At St. Tola's Church, there stands a beautifully sculptured Romanesque doorway from which projects twelve human heads and seven animal heads. The present church dates from the twelfth century but is built on the site of an earlier Christian monastery founded by St. Tola of Clonard in the eight century. In the chancel of the church there is a stone erected in 1684 which marks the resting place of Joan O'Dea, wife of Michael O'Dea, the last O'Dea chieftain. Inscribed are the Latin words:

Est Commune mor: Mors nulli pancit: honore debilis et fortis veneunt ad funere mortis.
Death comes to all without regard for station,
Weak and strong all come to the funeral pyre of death.

It was the O'Dea clan under their chieftain Conor that sent English lordship in what is now Clare to an 'early funeral pyre of death' at the decisive battle of Dysert O'Dea. Norman forces under Richard de Clare marched into the heart of Thomond with about 600 horses and 2,000 foot soldiers. He divided his army into three bodies. He brought the third body to Dysert, the seat of the O'Deas who were vassals to Muircheartach O'Brien, King of Thomond and rebel against the crown. Refused homage, de Clare's forces plundered cattle as they arrived, and on the morning of 10th May 1318 they came across a party of O'Deas rounding up their livestock at a ford on the stream, where Macken Bridge now stands. De Clare, falling into a trap, pursued the fleeing tribesmen over the ford with some of his knights and thus separated himself from his main body of troops. The awaiting O'Deas fell upon his knights and cut them to pieces, de Clare himself slain by the axe of the O'Dea. The leaderless invaders were eventually routed and Clare was free of foreign influence for another two centuries.

Dysert O'Dea

Tomás O'Maoldomhnaigh

Gesticulating to the world, above the south-facing circular doorway of the fourteenth century *Cill Inghine Baoithe*, the Church of the Daughter of Baoith is a crudely carved female figure euphemistically known as Sheela-na-Gig. It is the only instance of such a carving appearing above the entrance doorway of a church. Its ugly demeanour, its bulging eyes and its exposed genitalia, make this female exhibitionist figure uneasy on the eye, but one cannot deny that Sheela has a personality. It has engaged the Irish psyche since its introduction to these shores, which is attributed to Anglo-Norman influences.

Such stone-carved figures appeared on European pilgrimage routes as a warning against lust. Pilgrimages, like at Santiago de Compostela in northwestern Spain, were infamous for prostitutes that plied their trade along the route. They usually appeared on ecclesiastical buildings when first introduced in Ireland. The fact that they appeared on fortified buildings in a later period indicates a shifting in the interpretation of Sheelas by Irish society and perhaps a fusion between Norman and Gaelic influences.

During an enjoyable stint at the National Museum, I spent some time in the company of the Sheelas stored in the crypt, while carrying out a research project under the auspices of Ned Kelly, Keeper of Irish Antiquities. All I can vouch for is that after a number of days spent at this, one emerges onto the streets of the Capital with a more enlightened perspective on life!

This Church at Kilnaboy is also the only example in the whole of northwestern Europe with a double-armed cross built into its west gable. This type of cross, the Lorraine Cross, perhaps indicates the former presence here of a reliquary of the True Cross. Nearby is a well-preserved forge, where the Curtis family were blacksmiths. They were reputed to have possessed healing powers with animals which date back to antiquity. It was from this forge that pike heads were made for the ill-fated 1799 United Irishman's Rebellion in Clare.

Sheela-na-Gig, Kilnaboy

With its dramatic, stunning vistas that assail the senses, Cathair Chomáin is one of the finest archaeological attractions in Clare. Located between Carron and Kilnaboy, one walks a marked pathway for about a mile before ascending to the general plateau. From here a short stroll inland brings you to the site of the well-known trivallate cashel of Cathair Chomáin, perched on the edge of a ravine. A National Monument, it is the only ring-fort in the Burren yet to have been scientifically excavated, under the O'Neill-Hencken led Harvard Archaeological Expedition to Ireland in 1934.

An extended family of forty to fifty inhabitants probably lived here. Until recent times the extended family unit was a renowned feature of Clare's population structure. This *derbfhine* (true-group or kin-group) was heavily involved in wool processing, as demonstrated by the evidence of the excavation of shears, stone and bone spindle whorls and pin-beaters from the site and recent research. Over 4,000 kg of cattle bones were excavated from here as well and give an indication of the importance of livestock in the local economy. They would seem to confirm the traditional view of the ring-fort dwellers of the Burren as cattle ranchers. The numbers of querns discovered here also convey the practice of tillage in the locality. This Burren community lived here between the sixth and tenth centuries A.D.

There is much folklore attached to the area. It is claimed that the early Irish historical version of Viagra flows from the Seven Streams of Teeskagh, *Seacht Srotha na Teascaighe*, which is a beautiful natural feature at the base of the Cathair Chomáin cliffs. Its true meaning, *seven streams of the overflowing* is said to have originated from a wager placed on the mythical Spanish cow *Glas Gaibhneach*, brought to Ireland by Lon MacLoimtha, the legendary one legged, three handed Tuatha de Dannan blacksmith. The cow was known for her ample milk supply which, it was claimed, would fill any vessel, no matter what size. A canny punter milked her into a sieve and it flowed through to form the seven streams which form the striking feature seen today.

Cathair Chomáin

A teacher, Michael Cusack knew
The lesson learned at Waterloo:
"My victory," said Wellington,
"On Eton's playing-fields was won."
So Ireland's freedom would be gained
When Ireland's sons played Ireland's games.

Criostoir O'Flynn

Twenty five beating, driven hearts storm onto the hallowed turf of Croke Park to a cacophony of a thunderous, primeval roar and a blaze of colour which only 80,000 expectant Irish in one of the world's finest stadiums can produce. They will engage a national and global audience of millions over, for the next seventy minutes in a manly tussle for supremacy against an opposing county, that probably, like them, have spent five to six days a week for over ten months preparing for combat on the hurling or football fields of Ireland. This labour has now culminated in them appearing on All-Ireland final day.

And then it would be over, yet for both the victor and the vanquished they share a common thread, a thread that has run through the communal organisation of the G.A.A. for almost one hundred and twenty years. They have played and won and lost for the love of the game and in that they are truly amateurs, in the purest sense of the word and in that sense only, in this the era of modern professional sport. And in this they are linked umbillically to the great ghosts of the game, to the men and women who have coached juveniles, lined pitches, washed jerseys, promoted the matches and administered the game. These players and those before them have lived the dream that was first born in the heart of one of Clare's greatest sons, Michael Cusack of Carron. From this cottage came an architect of a nation.

Cusack was a superb athlete (accomplished in both rugby and cricket), brilliant scholar and renowned educator, and upon setting up a civil service academy in Dublin for tutoring potential recruits for state service, he immersed himself in the Gaelic renaissance that was emerging at the time in Irish society. His involvement with the Council of the Gaelic Union led to his conviction that Gaelic Games should be restored to their rightful place as a national sport. With this in mind, Cusack both summoned and opened the first meeting of the Gaelic Athletic Association in Hayes' Hotel, Thurles on November 1st 1884.

Michael Cusack

Tomás O'Maoldomnaiġ

Magh Adhair

On the east of Hell River, just over a mile and a half due east from the contented, equestrian village of Quin, one happens upon a complex of monuments and sites dating from prehistoric times through to the Middle Ages. The eye is instinctively drawn to the almost natural amphitheatre in the low-lying hollow. This large flat-topped mound, four metres high with a 29 metre diameter was most likely, by the Early Christian period, the royal inauguration place and location of the sacred tree of the predecessors of the O'Briens, the Uí Toirdealbhaith, the ruling sept of the Dal gCais. This is Magh Adhair.

By the eleventh century the O'Briens had risen from being an obscure Dalcassian clan before the fifth century A.D. to the high-kingship of Ireland under Brian Boru. Regarded by envious contemporaries as upstarts with a dubious pedigree, the O'Briens may have found it useful to link themselves with the vestiges of ancient power. This, Magh Adhair had in abundance and its mound, its standing stone, its association with water and its sacred tree are all diagnostic of an important inauguration site.

Magh Adhair, now associated with a small field, was once held as a large plain. The O'Brien was sometimes referred to as the Lord of Magh Adhair, and his kingdom, the Land of Magh Adhair and, almost invariably, the MacNamara inaugurated him. The inauguration of the princes of Thomond continued here to at least 1570 and an oireacht or gathering, continued here until the Great Famine when this practice, like so many others, died out during this shattering time.

There are other monuments in the vicinity such as the large nineteenth century cashel, most likely a royal residence and the possibly Iron Age hill fort in Ballyhickey. The ceremonial monument at Coogaun from c.2400B.C. testifies to the practice of prehistoric ritual around Magh Adhair.

Tomás O'Maoldomhnaigh

People and Place

Innovation is a recurring theme in Clare history. From the earliest recorded activities of the county's first inhabitants, the Mesolithic people, over 8,000 years ago, right up to the twentieth century development of the Shannon Duty Free Zone, the ability to improvise has been a hallmark of the people of Uí Floinn and Uí Caisin, Uí Fearmaic and Uí Chormaic, Uí Donghaile and Uí Conghaile, Uí Toirdealbhaith and Uí Ainmire, Uí Ronghaile and Uí Cearnaigh, Glenomra, Tuath Echtge and Tradraighe, Corca Baiscinn, East and West, Ibrickane, Burren and Corcomroe.

It is a land that has nurtured both visionary and inventor. Cornelius O'Brien of Birchfield House in Liscannor, one of the first to grasp the concept of Irish tourist potential, embraced his theories by developing his lands to cater for visitors in the 1830s. The result was the provision of O'Brien's Tower at the Cliffs of Moher, Clare's most visited attraction today, along with pathways, stables, round tables and a piper to entertain visitors. Unfortunately the piper one day fell over the cliffs while drunk, but traditional music still carries in the breezy airs of Moher today, as Clare County Council and Shannon Development, the mid-western semi-state development agency, vie with each other and with planning legislators over the establishment of a contemporary visitors centre at the Cliffs of Moher.

O'Brien's fellow Liscannor native, the inventor John Philip Holland was to change the course of modern warfare, as the father-founder of today's submarine. His Holland VI model, which used a gasoline engine on the surface and electric motors under water for propulsion, was commissioned into the United States Navy on

12th October 1900. Educated at Ennistymon Christian Brothers School and reared during a decade of famine, he emigrated to Boston carrying with him submarine designs in which the Irish American Clan na Gael leadership saw potential in a covert war against Britain's powerful fleet. However a rift developed amongst the Fenians over the use of the submarine and eventually the disillusioned Holland ended the great Irish 'Salt Water Enterprise'. He later did sell his designs to the US and Japanese navies and ironically to the very power he had originally intended to employ the submarine against, the Royal Navy. It was in 1904 that Holland told fellow inventor Thomas A. Edison that submarines would serve to end naval warfare, because they were so lethal. When he died in August 1914 the Great War had just begun and during it the lethal potential of Holland's submarine was realised.

Another Clare man who was to have a profound if a more positive impact on trans-Atlantic routes was Brendan O'Regan. An innovative, intelligent, well-travelled, energetic individual and of a political heritage, he made an indelible impression on all who had met him, even from his youngest days as manager at the Old Ground Hotel, Ennis and the Falls Hotel, Ennistymon. It was during his turn around of the ailing St. Stephen's Green Club in Dublin during WWII that he first came to the attention of the then Minister of Industry and Commerce, Seán Lemass. De Valera was anxious to have Irish people operate the catering facility at the flying boat base at Foynes and O'Regan was headhunted by Lemass for the job. When WWII ended shortly after he had taken up this job, Shannon Airport opened and O'Regan was appointed as Comptroller of Sales and Catering by Lemass to develop airport business under his [O'Regan's] own company, Sales and Catering Limited. This unique public-private partnership made Brendan O'Regan 'a one-man state company', as memorably quoted in Brian Callanan's *Ireland's Shannon Story.*

Thus began a golden period of dynamic growth at Shannon. O'Regan began selling Irish products to passengers at Shannon, many of whom were in transit during refuelling stopover flights. At this time, Lemass's department secured the passage of the 'customs free zone' for Shannon, making it the first 'free airport' in the world and since emulated by international airports globally. By the 1950s O'Regan's company was a success, opening up a mail order department, employing 500 people and having a £1.5 million annual turnover. Shannon was buzzing.

O'Regan was savvy enough to know that the emergence of long-haul aircraft would impact upon Shannon as a refuelling stop despite the government's commitment towards building a new jet runway there. He sought to improvise and diversify business at Shannon Airport with Lemass's backing in spite of the resistance of an unwieldy but influential minority of the Department of Industry and Commerce's otherwise progressive civil servants. A number of this unimaginative minority had sought to take over implementation of new developments at Shannon. O'Regan and his track record had managed to convince Lemass that the civil service structure lacked the flexibility, innovation and local autonomy to continue Shannon's growth, with the result that O'Regan's company was granted wider functions and thus was born the Shannon Free Airport Development Authority (later incorporated as SFADCo). O'Regan's leadership, motivation, team building, courage and belief all vindicated Lemass's call and the business interests of the mid-west were pulled together in developing industry, air freight and passengers, tourism and housing in the Shannon region. 'We must reach up into the sky and pull the business down' O'Regan said. Shannon's story became one of success and O'Regan's vision, combined with progressive state backing and encouragement, lay at its heart. It remains today as the economic pulse of Clare and the Mid West.

It was the Irishman of the Century, T.K. Whitaker and his White Paper on economic expansion in Ireland that informed the government thinking of his day. This laid the foundation for Shannon's development. As Secretary of the Department of Finance, Whitaker laid down the blueprint for Irish economic development in the *First Programme for Economic Expansion*, published in 1958. It is the county's proud claim that this venerated public servant is of Clare parentage.

Before the advent of Whitaker's economic plans, probably the greatest state project was undertaken some 30 years previous at Ardnacrusha in southeast Clare. The harnessing of the River Shannon was truly a People's Project, a statement of intent by the fledgling Irish Free State. The Shannon River Power Development Scheme and the resultant rural electrification had a great impact upon the economic and social life of the countryside.

A young Irish engineer, Dr T. A. McLaughlin, initiated these hydroelectric works, the first and largest project of its kind in Ireland. Its estimated cost at £5,200,000, about one-fifth of the government's annual expenditure in the mid 1920s, did initially raise eyebrows in Oireachtas debates but the proposal of using the mighty Shannon River for electrical generation caught the imagination of the people. This is reflected in the contemporary paintings of Seán Keating who depicted the various construction scenes, carried out by the contracted German engineering firm, Siemens-Schuckert, between 1925 and 1929. *His Night's Candles Burnt Out* captures the essence of communal solidarity of this time.

The construction of a special railway branch line from Limerick, the opening of work camps such as at Ardnacrusha (which housed 750 men), Clonlara and at O'Brien's Bridge and the employment of over 5000 men, skilled and labourers, all indicate the major scale of this mighty civil engineering project. In this undertaking, a seven and a half mile canal was constructed beside the Shannon for the purpose of directing some of its water into the giant turbines at Ardnacrusha to transform its energy into electricity. From the Ardnacrusha station, a tailrace one-mile canal was to lead the water back into the Shannon above Limerick city. The project was also to generate such national and international interest that it became a visitor attraction with over 250,000 estimated sightseers witnessing the construction. In Clare was taken the first step towards national electrification and a young Irish engineer's vision was realised.

The storied landscape of Clare has inspired the vision and actions of its people from antiquity up to the present day. A classic case in hand is embodied in the life of Michael Greene whose recent untimely departure from this world has surely enhanced the next. He came from an hotelier background, managing Hyland's Hotel in Ballyvaughan. In an interview published posthumously in the *World of Hibernia* magazine, Greene recounted an epiphany he experienced one day looking out at the limestone hills and plateaux of his beloved Burren country. He saw Cahermacnaughten and in his mind's eye its great Brehon law school of the past once held under the auspices of the O'Davorens. Cahermacnaughten was the Harvard or Yale of the old Gaelic order. He decided from this moment, with the help of his wife Mary, to recapture the Burren's ancient standing as a centre of learning. To this effect and after an arduous odyssey, he founded and became a Director of the internationally acclaimed Burren College of Art at Newtown Castle. It hosts several national and international conferences each year including the Brehon Law School and the Archaeological and Historical weekend. The college eventually became affiliated with N.U.I. Galway. It also served to copper-fasten Ballyvaughan's standing as a tourist destination. Greene passed away playing football for his beloved Ballyvaughan aged 44. The college Dean, Paul Gregg, said of Greene

> *"He had the mind of a giant. He stood tall in Ballyvaughan, the height of his vision clearing the mountain tops of the Burren. He recognised paths leading forward in distant lands. His dreams for the community were not fleeting but steadfast, strengthened by robust determination."*

Another group of Clare people, whose minds have been illuminated by the spirit that did illustrate the O'Davoren manuscripts of the twelfth century, is Comhar Conradh na Boirne Teo, a group of people from New Quay, Carron and Kilfenora who joined together to form a co-operative society that was affiliated with ICOS in 1973. In 1975 it pioneered what was then a novel concept of establishing an interpretative centre for the Burren region. Such a centre was unique for its era and the first facility of its kind in the country. The Burren Display Centre in Kilfenora stands as a tribute to the foresight and dynamism of the original shareholders of Comhar Conradh na Boirne. One of the members of this steering committee was Brian Mooney. A poetic visionary, he saw in his surrounds, resources that could be utilised in bringing the beauty and essence of the Burren country to a larger audience. He initiated the renowned Burren Perfumery in Carron, Ireland's oldest, over 30 years ago to some degree of scepticism, but its continued use of natural products in the traditional method of perfume making and the desire of companies such as Aer Lingus to carry it has helped the business to carve a niche for itself in today's market.

Clare is very much an island county and its turbulent past has helped to form its distinct personality. There seems to be a form of magnetism between its people and charismatic leaders, which can be traced back to the time of probably Ireland's greatest leader, Brian Boru. Born in 941A.D. to the Dalcassian chieftain, Cinnéide, of the clan Uí Toirdealbhaith in the east of Clare, and Bé Bhionn, daughter of the king of West Connaught, Brian came into an Irish world that was racked by Viking wars and inter-tribal feuding. Both the death of his father at the hands of the Vikings and his brother Mahon's assassination by rival chieftains must have had a profound impact on him and his outlook. It had been with Mahon that Brian led a band of dissident warriors against the might of the Vikings in the mountains of East Clare. They had spectacular successes, such as the recovery of the royal Munster capital of Cashel from the 'Land leapers'.

Their power grew to such an extent that one year after Mahon's assassination, Brian, as the new chieftain of the Dalcassians, was inaugurated as the King of Munster. The 36-year-old King continued to take the war to the Vikings while also pacifying Munster chieftains. He was a mould breaker, ruling Munster from his Killaloe stronghold instead of the traditional Cashel capital and he soon cast his ambitious eye of the High Kingship of Ireland, which in theory had always been the preserve of the Uí Neill. The High King Malachy decided to mark Brian's cards by invading Thomond and cutting down the sacred inauguration tree at Magh Adhair, the greatest insult he could make to Brian and his kingdom.

For the next fifteen years, there followed a great power struggle between the two leaders. It ended with a mutual pact to divide Ireland between them in 997. This led to the Battle of Gleann Máma in Wicklow where the erstwhile rivals combined to rout the forces of

Maolmordha, King of Leinster, and his Viking allies. This, however, and the strategic political marriages that followed (Brian married the siren like Gormflhlaith, the defeated Leinster king's sister and Malachy's ex-wife, and to her son Sitric, the Viking overlord of Dublin, was given Boru's daughter in marriage) further strengthened Brian's hand, to the point where he forced Malachy's abdication in 1002, becoming the first Munster king to assume the high kingship of Ireland.

For the next 12 years Brian reigned as High King from Kincora, where today now stands the Catholic church of Killaloe, and it was to here that the great chieftains of Ireland came to pay homage and give 'hostages' to Clare's greatest son. Recognising the importance of naval strength, he commanded fleets at Lough Derg and at Limerick. His ships from Dublin, Waterford and Cork extracted tribute along the Welsh coast and from Argyll in Scotland.

Brian proved himself a strong king, tactful and respected. He continued his shrewd pursuit of dynastic marriages from which one, the marriage of his daughter to Malcolm II of Scotland, every Scottish and English sovereign from the union of the two crowns in 1603 could trace their descent. He encouraged the commerce that successive Viking settlers had built up, restored churches and fortifications and patronised the arts. In 1005 he visited Armagh and endorsed its Church's primacy over Ireland.

It was in the *Book of Armagh* that Brian was referred to as 'Imperatoris Scotorum', Emperor of the Gael. His policies and reforms, achieved during the autumn of his life, have ensconced his name in all that is forever Ireland. Not even the axe with which the fleeing Viking Brodar felled the 73 year old Brian after his greatest triumph at the Battle of Clontarf on Good Friday 1014, the battle that forever broke Viking power in Ireland, could cut down Boru's legacy as the

> *'over king of the Irish of Ireland and of the foreigners and of the Britons, the Augustus of the whole of north-west Europe.'*

With the exiled Wild Geese and Clare's Dragoons went the Jacobite leaders of the county, following the wars of the seventeenth century. In the new order agrarian protest became a distinctive feature of rural society, from the eras of the Houghers, Whiteboys and Rightboys to the Ribbonmen, Rockites and Terry Alts of the early nineteenth century. The agrarian violence committed by these movements such as destruction of property or livestock, or the beating, mutilation or killing of 'offenders' was traditionally seen as reflecting the alienation of the Catholic Gaelic peasantry. Assassination became more commonplace in the wake of the repression of the United Irishmen in the 1790s and the outbreaks of unrest were reactions to developments such as enclosure of common land, tithes and levies as well as agricultural depression and falling prices. It was only when Famine gripped the land that these societies petered out in Ireland but it was their discontent that helped to motor Daniel O'Connell's Catholic Association.

Daniel O'Connell, a Kerry Catholic landowner, first came to political prominence through his opposition to the Act of Union. From 1805 he was a stalwart of the movement for Catholic emancipation. His strong opposition to the Veto, which gave the Crown greater influence over the Catholic Church, along with his fame as a barrister, made O'Connell a popular champion and with the introduction of the Catholic Rent, the Catholic Association became a mass movement of the people. It was Charles Patrick O'Gorman Mahon from Ennis, known to history as the O'Gorman Mahon, who successfully convinced O'Connell to put this support to the test in Clare and run for Parliament against Vesey Fitzgerald in 1828. O'Connell was overwhelmingly voted in by the Clare electorate, a number of whom ran the risk of eviction for doing so. This famous victory paved the way for Catholic emancipation and representation in parliament.

The O'Gorman Mahon became a forerunner of the modern campaign manager during this election. He developed elaborate tactics such as when O'Connell and his supporters were forbidden to stand on the courthouse balcony in Ennis to address the public. In response to this dictate, the O'Gorman Mahon promptly suspended himself from the balcony with a rope and proceeded to address the assembly. Shortly afterwards The O'Gorman Mahon was opposed by O'Connell when he put himself forward for election against Major McNamara in 1831. His subsequent defeat made him henceforth an embittered enemy of O'Connell. He forsook politics and became an adventurer and soldier for the next forty years.

His travels took him from France and Russia (where he earned the favour of both King Louis Philippe and the Tsar) to China and India where he fought against the Tartars. He was a Governor General in the Uruguayan Civil War, a commander in the Chilean Navy in the war against Spain, a colonel in the Brazilian army and he fought with the Union in the American Civil War. Before his great odyssey ended he had become intimate with Bismarck and the German Crown Prince and had befriended Louis Napoleon. Truly Stanley Kubrick's Barry Lyndon, the epic Hollywood depiction of a fictional Irish military adventurer who fought in European continental engagements for a variety of realms, would pale in comparison to this gentleman soldier's life. Yet there was still another chapter in this remarkable man's life. He returned to the Irish political stage as a Home Ruler and in 1879 he was elected MP for Clare, a position he held for the next six years. Before his death at 91 years of age in 1891, he still retained in him the passion to oppose Parnell during the rancorous split in the Home Rule movement. His remains lie in the O'Connell plot at Glasnevin Cemetery and with his death died the exuberant ways of a past era.

A fellow Clare contemporary of The O'Gorman Mahon and a man who was to have a great impact upon 'advanced' nationalism in Ireland was William Smith O'Brien. Descended from the line of Boru, he received a Cambridge education and was actually elected as a Tory MP for Ennis, but supported Catholic Emancipation. He became convinced that Ireland could not progress until it broke the union with Britain and to this end he became a leading member of the Repeal Association, acting as leader during O'Connell's imprisonment in 1844. In 1846 he sided with the hawkish Young Irelanders, Duffy, Meagher and Mitchell and broke with O'Connell. In his last speech to the House of Commons, he warned that Britain would soon be faced by an Irish republic. Having put himself at the head of the Young Irelander's abortive rebellion of 1848, he was arrested, and sentenced to be hanged, drawn and quartered but this sentence was commuted to exile to Tasmania. He later received an unconditional pardon and returned to Ireland in 1856, playing no further role in politics up to his death in 1864.

It was the advanced nationalism of the Young Irelanders that informed the Fenian revolutionary movement of a decade later. The Fenian movement had taken off in Clare when Edmond O'Donovan, son of the Irish scholar and historian John O'Donovan from Broadford, swore in John Clune of Carrahan, Quin, as head of the movement in Clare while he was organising Fenian cells throughout the country. After the Fenian Rising of 1867, Clune, who had succeeded in helping to make Clare one of the staunchest Fenian counties, was sentenced to be hanged, but this too was commuted to transportation, in this case Bermuda. He escaped to the USA where he became a founder member of the Claremen's Association in New York in 1887 and was elected its first chairman. It was Brian Clune, his brother, who assumed the Clare Fenian leadership until his enforced exile to New York in 1891. He once claimed that he had administered the Fenian oath to William Redmond.

Major Willie Redmond represented East Clare at Westminster for over a quarter of a century, from the Parnellite split to his soldier's death on the Western Front during the Great War. He was a charismatic figure; very popular with his constituents from the time Clare bucked the national trend and came out in favour of the two Parnellite candidates, Rochford Maguire and Redmond. He once told his constituents from the 'moonlight county' during a period of agrarian agitation that he had 'done a lot of queer things in my life but I have never yet driven a bullock' to rapturous laughter. He viewed armed rebellion as futile and sincerely believed that a united Home Rule Ireland could exist at peace within an Empire that he saw as being as much Irish as it was British. He gave his life for his idealism but with his passing died also the world of constitutionalism in Clare. It was to make way for the active forces of revolution.

When the sole surviving commandant of the Easter Rising of 1916, Eamon de Valera, won the famous by-election of 1917, caused by

Redmond's death, it marked the changing of the guard. De Valera represented revolution and the democratic majority of East Clare made him their representative. It was a watershed election that confirmed the arrival of both Eamon de Valera and Sinn Féin on the political stage. Lord Wimborne, the Lord Lieutenant of Ireland wrote to the British cabinet in the wake of this result:

> *The Sinn Féin victory in East Clare is a fact of cardinal significance and has precipitated events . . . the fact remains that in a remarkably well conducted political contest, sustained by excellent candidates on both sides, the electors on a singularly frank issue of self government within the Empire versus an Independent Irish Republic have overwhelmingly pronounced for the latter.*

The stunning victory electrified the country and gave renewed impetus to the republican movement throughout Clare and Ireland. At the general election of December 1918, the outgoing East Clare member, Eamon de Valera, now president of the political and military wings of the republican movement was returned unopposed. The political association of Eamon de Valera with the Banner County was to last until 1959. During his long career, he cast the largest shadow of them all over twentieth century Ireland and while his name was capable of evoking both love and hate throughout the country, nobody could be indifferent towards him. During his 42-year representation of Clare there was an obvious rapport between de Valera and the people and they supported him en masse again when he ran for President in 1959. Many personal accounts and memoirs from both friend and foe have referred to his aura of dignity, integrity and leadership and this was a major factor in his ability to command such loyalty from his followers and from the party he founded, Fianna Fáil. From New York to Bruree, from Mweeloon to Lincoln prison, from Feakle to the Dáil and the League of Nations, de Valera was a chief of men.

Just when de Valera was taking up residency at Áras an Uachtaráin, a young medical doctor from Miltown Malbay was assuming the ministerial post for Education. Dr Patrick J. Hillery had previously served as Fianna Fáil T.D. for Clare for eight consecutive years from 1951. His innovative approach as Education Minister prepared the way for the introduction of comprehensive schools, regional technical colleges and higher technical education. Recently released papers from the National Archives detailed how Hillery as Minister for Foreign Affairs held secret meetings in the North during the developing crisis in Northern Ireland, feeling that there was a genuine threat of civil war. He also successfully led the negotiations for Irish entry into the European Economic Community in 1973 following which he became Ireland's first European Commissioner. He relinquished this post when approached by Fianna Fáil to become President of Ireland by all party consensus in December 1976, in the wake of Cearbhall Ó Dálaigh's resignation. He was returned unopposed seven years later. Paddy Hillery retired from public life when his second term of office expired. Upon a motion of North Clare councillors, the library in his native Miltown was named after him and they also mooted the creation of a Presidential Hall in the town. It would be a fitting tribute to a man of his people.

Golf was one of Dr Hillery's passions having grown up near the historic Spanish Point course and in Clare there are some magnificent courses whether it be the East Clare, the newly opened, Greg Norman designed Doughmore or Lahinch. The latter two are generally accepted in golfing circles as being amongst the most challenging golf links in the world. The famed South of Ireland Championship was inaugurated at Lahinch in 1895 and is the oldest match play championship in the country.

Clare is a sporting paradise for those who enjoy outdoor pursuits and whether it be shark fishing off Black Head, angling for game, sea and coarse, surfing around Doughmore and Lahinch, hiking, caving, cycling, horse riding, relaxing with island boat trips to the Aran Islands, Scattery and Holy Islands, dolphin watching trips from Carrigaholt and Kilrush, leisurely Shannon cruises from Killaloe, or just simply taking in a championship club game in hurling or football (there are sixty clubs in the Clare), the county is amply provided for. If there are those who want to get in touch with their Neolithic past, they can even try their hand at the world stone throwing championships held here annually.

The many fine, atmospheric restaurants of Clare, with imaginative chefs, as highlighted by the Clare Good Food Circle, reap the bountiful harvest of the sea to provide regional culinary delights, and monkfish, bass and trout are specialities in many of these eating-houses. Vernacular foods can also be sampled on festive occasions such as the Carrigaholt Oyster Festival. Another culinary feature of Clare are the famous Burren Lamb dishes served up throughout the county, with its inviting taste, a product of the sweet pasturages of the Burren. Mionnán, or goat is another trademark regional dish served up in the Burren at hostelries such as Cassidys, whose proprietors once may have hit hard in football, but also know how to entertain. Indeed it is an increasing trend for Clare restaurants to select their foods from local suppliers offering indigenous produce, such as duck, pheasant, lamb, cheeses and jams. Some Clare farmers have shown the courage and innovation to diversify their traditional methods so as to remain viable in the ever-tightening European market, supported by development bodies such as the Clare County Enterprise Board and Leader.

Such a departure can be seen as part of the movement to preserve a way of life during a time of increasing urbanisation and shifting demographics due to economic and planning pressures. Although the population of Clare now stands at over 100,000 for the first time in ninety years, and the Celtic tiger has devoured the troughs of emigration, many parts of rural Clare are still haemorrhaging its lifeblood, as the trend is now firmly fixed on concentrated movement from rural areas to the larger towns and their environs. For example, the population of Clare jumped by almost 10% from 1996 to 2002 but the most substantial part of this growth is reflected in the 25% increase of the Ennis urban area, and 36% growth of the Ennis Rural area. These trends are a challenge for Clare society as a whole and not just for Irish planning departments or latest EU planning initiatives.

Clare society has always been jealous of its individuality and yet open to innovation. This has been reflected in its embracing of technology, with Ennis standing as the Information Age Town of Ireland, and new technological parks have been announced for Ennis and Shannon. The knowledge society is the buzzword in economic parlance today and Clare is to the forefront of the development of this technological industry in Ireland, with sound infrastructure and a highly trained, motivated and skilled workforce. It is they who have been bequeathed the knowledge of previous generations, a knowledge that, although not quantifiable by today's marketing or economic gauges, had wisdom, soul and wit, a respect for life and landscape and reverence for tradition. It is this grounding that puts Clare in an advantageous position to carve a niche for itself in the international market of the knowledge society.

At the heart of Ireland's Mid West, Clare is both acclaimed for its modern vibrancy and venerated for its ancient and recent past. Síle de Valera, in her recent post as Minister for Arts, Heritage, Gaeltacht and the Islands, has contributed enormously to the cultural enhancement of the county with her support of many capital projects. Clare today stands as a port of hope to a new wave of economic refugees, as history comes full circle, and with responsible governance, they too with their drive, hunger and respective cultures, will embellish Clare society. It is said in the ancient prophecies of St. Colmcille that before the end of days Ireland will be amongst the greatest of nations. If this does come to pass, Clare and its people will ensure that such a nation will continue to have spirituality and wisdom, innovation and motivation. And yes, the craic.

Beidh an Lámh Láidir in Uachtar.

Bibliography

Béaloideas 1996-1997, Journal of the Folklore of Ireland Society.
Brennan, P., *Clare - Unique images of the artist's native County Clare*, Dublin 2002.
Butler, R., ed., *St. Flannan's 1891-1981*, Clare 1981.
Byrnes, O., *Against The Wind, Memories of Clare Hurling*, Cork 1996.
Callanan, B., *Ireland's Shannon Story*, Dublin 2000.
Clare Association Yearbook 2003, Dublin 2003.
County Clare Patriotic Benevolent and Social Association of New York, *An Clár Abú, From Clare to Here*, New York 1988.
Connolly, J.S., ed. *The Oxford Companion to Irish History*, New York 1998.
Coogan, T.P., *Wherever Green is Worn*, United Kingdom 2000.
Cronin, D., *Dysert O' Dea, A History Trail*
Cunningham, G., *Burren Journey West*, Limerick 1980.
Curry, E., O'Donovan J., *The Antiquities of County Clare*, Clare 1997.
Dal gCais 1979, 1991.
Danaher, K., *The Year in Ireland - Irish Calendar Customs*, Cork 1972.
Dillon, T., ed., *The Banner*, New York 1963.
Dolan, T. P., *A Dictionary of Hiberno-English*, Dublin 1999.
Ennistymon Parish Magazine
Feehan, M. J., *The Secret Places of the Burren*, Dublin 1987.
Galvin, Br. Rev., *Cameos of Historic Clare.*
Grenham, J., *An Illustrated History of Ireland*, Dublin 1997.
Guerin, H., Rynne C., Buttimer N., *The Heritage of Ireland*, Cork 2000.
Lawton, T., *Walking Ireland*, Dublin 1998.
Lewis, S., *Co. Clare, A History and Topography*, Clare 1995.
Lillis, K., *Kieran Lillis Remembers Stories of Life in Rural Ireland*, Clare 1994.
MacNeill, Marie *The Festival of Lughnasa*, Oxford 1962
Madden, G., *A History of Tuamgraney and Scariff*, Clare 2000.

Maher, P., *An East Clare Landscape Adventure*, Geographical Survey of Ireland 1998.
McCarthy, D., *Ireland's Banner County - Clare From the Fall of Parnell to the Great War 1890-1918,* Clare 2002.
McInerney, T., *Kilkee,* Clare 2000.
McNamara, Sean, *The Burren Wonderland*, Clare
Newman, R. Chatterton, *Brian Boru, King of Ireland*, Dublin 1986.
Ó Cillín, P.S., *Ballads of Co. Clare 1850-1976,* Galway 1976.
Ó Cillín, P.S., *Traveller's in Co. Clare 1459-1843,* Galway 1977.
Ó hAllmharáin, G., *A pocket history of Irish Traditional Music*, Dublin 1998.
O'Connell, W. J., Korff, A., eds., *The Book of the Burre*n, Galway 1991.
Ó Dálaigh, B., ed., *Corporation Book of Ennis*, Dublin 1990.
O Dálaigh, B., *The Stranger's Gaze Travels in County Clare 1534-1950,* Clare 1998.
Official Guide to Clare, Clare Local Studies Centre.
Studia Hibernica, 1974 Vol. 14.
Ó Murchadha, C., *Sable wings over the land - Ennis Co. Clare, and it's wider community during the Great Famine*, Clare 1998.
Power J., *A history of Clare Abbey and Killone.*
Prestage, M., McGuigan, B., *Celtic Fists*, Great Britain 1997.
Sheedy K., *The Horses of Clare*, Ireland 2001.
Sheedy K., *The Clare Elections,* Dublin 1993.
Sherkin Island Marine Station - A beginner's Guide to Ireland's Seashore, Cork 1999.
Smith, J., *Ballads of the Banner,* Dublin 1998.
Spellissy, S., *The Ennis Compendium from Royal Dún to Information Age Town.*
Spellissy, S., *Clare County of Contrast*, Clare 1987.
Taylor, P., *The West Clare Railway*, Brighton 1994.
The Burren Way, Shannon Development.
The Mid Clare Way by the Mid Clare way Committee.
The Other Clare, Vols. 14, 16&19.
Weir, H., *The O'Brien's.*
Weir, H., *Houses of Clare*, Clare 1986.
Westropp, T.J., *Folklore of Clare*, Clare 2000.

Dear Reader

This book is from our much complimented illustrated book series which includes:-

Belfast
By the Lough's North Shore
East Belfast
South Belfast
Antrim, Town & Country
Inishowen
Donegal Highlands
Donegal, South of the Gap
Donegal Islands
Fermanagh
Omagh
Cookstown
Dundalk & North Louth
Drogheda & the Boyne Valley
Blanchardstown, Castleknock and the Park
Dundrum, Stillorgan & Rathfarnham
Blackrock, Dún Laoghaire, Dalkey
Limerick's Glory
Galway on the Bay
The Book of Clare
Armagh
Ring of Gullion
The Mournes
Heart of Down
Strangford Shores

For the more athletically minded our illustrated walking book series includes:-

Bernard Davey's Mourne
Bernard Davey's Mourne Part 2
Tony McAuley's Glens

Also available in our 'Illustrated History & Companion' Range are:-

City of Derry
Lisburn
Holywood
Banbridge
Ballymoney

And from our Music series:-

Colum Sands, Between the Earth and the Sky

We can also supply prints, individually signed by the artist, of the paintings featured in the above titles as well as many other areas of Ireland.

For details on these superb publications and to view samples of the paintings they contain, you can visit our web site at www.cottage-publications.com or alternatively you can contact us as follows:-

Telephone: +44 (028) 9188 8033 Fax: +44 (028) 9188 8063

Cottage Publications
is an imprint of
Laurel Cottage Ltd
15 Ballyhay Road
Donaghadee, Co. Down
N. Ireland, BT21 0NG